FIAMMA

THE ESSENCE OF CONTEMPORARY ITALIAN COOKING

Michael White
with Joanna Pruess

Desserts by Elizabeth Katz

Photography by Joseph De Leo

WILEY

John Wiley & Sons, Inc.

Published by John Wiley & Sons, Inc., Hoboken, New Jersey
Published simultaneously in Canada

Library of Congress Cataloging-in-Publication Data:

White, Michael, 1971–
 Fiamma : the essence of contemporary Italian cooking / Michael White with Joanna Pruess ; desserts by Elizabeth Katz ; photography by Joseph De Leo.
  p. cm.
 Includes index.
 ISBN-13: 978-0-7645-9931-6
 ISBN-10: 0-7645-9931-3 (cloth)
 1. Cookery, Italian. 2. Fiamma (Restaurant) I. Pruess, Joanna. II. Katz, Elizabeth, 1975- III. Title.
 TX723.W52 2006
 641.5945—dc22

                    2005033610

Printed in China

10 9 8 7 6 5 4 3 2 1

CONTENTS

vi   **FOREWORD BY JOHN MARIANI**

viii   **ACKNOWLEDGMENTS**

ix   **PREFACE**

xi   **INTRODUCTION**

1   Antipasti
       Antipasti

51   Paste, Polenta e Risotto
       Pasta, Polenta, and Risotto

101   Pesce
       Fish

137   Pollame e Carni
       Poultry and Meat

181   Le Verdure
       Vegetables

197   Dolci
       Desserts

251   Ricette di Base
       Staples

266   **SOURCES**

269   **INDEX**

Not too many years ago I was pretty resolute in believing

that a chef needed to be born and raised within the food culture that he tried to reproduce in his kitchen. It seemed patently obvious then—and still makes sense—that the best representatives of, say, Alsatian or Sicilian or Basque or Goan cuisine would come from those territories and had eaten the food since childhood. They absorbed the often sacrosanct social, cultural, and culinary traditions of the family, the tribe, the village, or the city. And, as a result, their rendering of Valencian paella or Russian pierogi or Norwegian lutefisk is not simply "authentic" but born of a lifetime of learning.

If any chef has caused me to rethink that paradigm it is Michael White, a big, self-effacing Midwestern American, born in Beloit, Wisconsin, who is the executive chef-partner of New York's fine Italian restaurant Fiamma and the author of this cookbook. White (his very name seems to exemplify meatloaf sandwiches and milk gravy!) was nineteen when he enrolled at Kendall Culinary School in Evanston, Illinois. He simultaneously worked at Chicago's Spiaggia restaurant under the great Italian-American chef Paul Bartolotta, who had made a pilgrimage to Italy to learn the secrets of true *cucina italiana* at the famous San Domenico restaurant outside of Bologna and had taken over as chef at that restaurant's New York offspring.

Bartolotta must have sensed something of himself in White, recommending that he too go to the Old World kitchens to learn the way things should be done if he were truly interested in pursuing a career in Italian restaurants. White took the challenge. For the next seven years, subsisting mostly on room and board—of course, the "board" in Italy is as good as it gets in the world—he learned the virtues of simplicity in Italian cooking along with its secrets and complexities. He discovered how to make gnocchi light as a feather, how to shop the seasonal market, and how to respect the culinary traditions of a region, a village, a trattoria, and a kitchen.

Along the way, White also apprenticed at San Domenico, under its famous chef Valentino Marcattilii, whose devotion to refining traditional Italian cooking into a very high form of cuisine left an indelible imprint. It would translate into White's own commitment to serve only the best and the freshest food as an extension of his own personality. In 1997, White proudly became Marcattilii's *Chef di Cucina,* which was both a challenge and great honor for an American— especially one without any Italian blood.

Furthering his career at notable *Michelin Guide's* star restaurants in France, like Le Moulin de Mougins and L'Oasis, White learned the precision and disciplines of the French classical kitchen. But his heart was obviously in Italy and, after further work as *Chef di Cucina* at Spiaggia, White was tapped by restaurateur Steve Hanson to come to New York as chef of Fiamma.

Every great American restaurateur seems to have an Italian restaurant in him that he needs to do. So Hanson, whose previous efforts include the gargantuan Blue Fin and Ruby Foo's in the Theater District, put his reputation on the line in opening Fiamma in SoHo. It was most certainly his biggest gamble, not because of its size, which was much smaller than his other crowd-driven restaurants, but because of the commitment to rigorously authentic Italian cuisine and wine of a kind rare even in New York. Paul Bartolotta had shown it could be done at San Domenico in

New York, as did the redoubtable Mario Batali at Babbo and Michael Cetrulo at Scalini Fedeli. But they had something of an edge by being Italian-American, growing up eating good Italian-American home cooking. Michael White had the experience but not the name, and he had a lot more to prove to finicky, demanding foodies and food critics, including me.

Yet White did it with flair and a dedication that seems almost ingenuous—what Italians call *sprezzatura,* the art of concealed art.

White incorporated everything he knew from long experience into Fiamma's menu, from dishes like red mullet with tiny tomatoes, arugula, and *salsa verde* to tiny ravioli stuffed with braised veal shank. It was all absolutely, positively right on the mark. And, in its generosity of proportions, Fiamma's food also had a definite and irrepressible American style that admirably manifested White's own midwestern roots.

White caused me to rethink my own ideas about Italian food in this country and, indeed, I named White "Chef of the Year" in my annual roundup of Best New Restaurants for *Esquire* magazine in 2002. This year, the fact that Fiamma is one of only four Italian restaurants in the city to receive the *Michelin Guide's* star rating seems to seal the reputation of both the restaurant and of White's tremendous talent.

When friends come to town and want an engaging, ebullient Italian restaurant with superb Italian food and New York vibes, I send them to Fiamma; when friends from Italy complain they cannot find food in New York the way it tastes in their country, I send them to Fiamma. They all come away amazed.

How difficult is it for White and his kitchen to reproduce the flavors and textures of true Italian food in the United States? Well, by starting with the best—often the most expensive—ingredients available in a city with nonpareil resources for delivering the goods, White can happily draw upon everything from the finest funghi porcini and white truffles to 100-year-old balsamic vinegar and elixir-like virgin olive oil.

Fortunately for the rest of us, such ingredients are, for the most part, pretty readily available from local markets or mail order. And thanks to Joanna Pruess' precise prose and supervision of the recipe development and testing, the reader of this cookbook can duplicate White's food with a reasonable expectation that it will taste as it does at Fiamma.

So I surrender my former insistence that a good Italian cook must grow up in the shade of an olive tree in Umbria or by the seashore at Bari. Michael White, true-blue American boy that he is, has learned what it takes to make great Italian food. This extends equally to Elizabeth Katz whose wonderful desserts are included here. Now, with this marvelous cookbook, so will you.

—John Mariani

Many people worked with me to produce this, my first cookbook.
My most sincere thanks go to all of them:

JOANNA PRUESS, my collaborator, for helping me to get organized, cajoling me into meeting deadlines, and so perfectly capturing my thoughts on paper. I could not have picked a better person with whom to work.

JANE DYSTEL, our agent, for championing this project, overseeing the proposal, and wisely presenting it to John Wiley & Sons.

The B.R. Guest team, starting with **STEPHEN HANSON,** for his belief in me, his total support, and for building beautiful restaurants that perfectly showcase my food.

ELIZABETH KATZ, our very talented pastry chef, although not Italian by heritage, she mastered and embraced some of the great classics as well as the spirit of what Italian *dolci* should be.

DONNA RODRIGUEZ, director of corporate communications, who keeps us all moving effectively in the right direction, along with **CHERYL PERL** for her public relations work with me and to **MICHELE LEE** for her wonderful cover design.

Our corporate executive chefs at B.R. Guest, **CHRIS GIARRAPUTO** and **BRETT REICHLER,** who support my efforts even when I don't follow the rules. Also in the kitchen: **CHRISTIAN FANTONI,** my chef de cuisine, **PEDRO CRUZ,** my right hand man at Fiamma, and all of my line cooks who have been with me since Day 1. And, the purveyors and farmers who work continuously to elevate the quality of the ingredients they bring to me.

DANIELE SBORDI, Fiamma's general manager and partner, for keeping all the balls in the air. And my front and back of the house team who do such an exceptional job of selling our food and serving it on a daily basis with unfailing professionalism.

I'd also like the thank the very talented team at Fiamma Las Vegas at the MGM Grand Hotel; notably **CARLOS BUSCAGLIA,** the executive chef and, **ALEX TAYLOR,** the general manager.

The B.R. Guest recipe tester team led by **MELISSA MANNERS** and **KATIE STAMARIS,** and including **STEFANIE ARCK, CAROLINE BISI, BARBARA CARLON, GRAHAM FISK, ERIC FUENTY, AMY KOYIADES, CARLY MASUCCI, TANYA MILLER, ELIZABETH NICOULIN, BRET PAIGE, RON RIEMER, TRACIE SIMON, JUDITH UBELHOER, JENNIFER ULRICH,** and **BLYTHE ZAVA.**

MELISSA GAMAN, DENISE MICKELSEN, and **MELISSA VAUGHAN,** three very talented professional recipe testers, whose dedication and intelligence throughout, but especially at the end, made even the most complicated recipes accessible to home cooks.

JUSTIN SCHWARTZ, our editor at Wiley, for his enthusiasm for this book, his fastidious attention to detail, and his intelligent suggestions; his conscientious staff, including: **CHRISTINE DICOMO** and **CHRISTINA SOLAZZO;** and publicity director **GYPSY LOVETT.** Also to **GINGER MCRAE** for her attentive and sensitive copy editing.

JOEY DE LEO's photographs that elegantly captured my food and **ANTHONY LEBERTO'S** food styling.

FRANCESCA MANESCO, for translating the recipe titles and appropriate terminology into Italian.

Chef **VALENTINO MARCATTILII** of San Domenico, my mentor, and chef **PAUL BARTOLOTTA,** who gave me my first job at Spiaggia, then gave me the opportunity to go work in Italy.

MARY ANN and **GERRY WHITE,** my parents. Thank you for exposing me to the most exceptional upbringing and values. My dad taught me the value of hard work, and my mom showed me that even gigantic problems are just small blips in the grand scheme of things.

GIOVANNA, my wife. Life wouldn't be worth it without you. Thanks for staying up every night until I get home.

FRANCESCA, my daughter, who always brings me joy.

Finally, to all the guests at Fiamma and Vento who have supported my efforts in the kitchen, befriended me, and encouraged me to write this book.

I am one of the luckiest people I know. Every day I get

to cook the kind of food I fell passionately in love with during seven incredible years in Italy.
I don't just eat these dishes at home with my Italian-born wife, Giovanna, and our daughter
Francesca, I am also the executive chef and partner of Fiamma, a well-regarded contemporary
Italian restaurant in Manhattan. There are other Fiammas in Las Vegas and Scottsdale, as well.

As a person of Norwegian heritage from Beloit, Wisconsin, I had never even tasted real
Italian cooking until I was nineteen years old. After culinary school, I went to work at Spiaggia,
a much honored Chicago restaurant, where suddenly *la cucina Italiana* gripped me as nothing
before. But I lacked both the cultural background and technical skills to approach it authentically
and decided a trip across the Atlantic was essential.

My time in Italy taught me about the ingredients, techniques, and traditions that have been
the foundations of Italian cooking for centuries. I also worked alongside talented chefs who, while
using these same foods and methods in a more contemporary style, always remained true to the
Italian idiom. As amazing as it sounds for someone born in America, I ended my time in Italy as
head chef at San Domenico, a Michelin two-starred restaurant in Imola, known for its
contemporary Italian cooking.

These positive experiences instilled a dream of recreating this style of cooking in America,
where stylish foods were prepared with mostly unadorned ingredients that taste like themselves.

When I came home, it was as chef de cuisine of Spiaggia. There I applied the ideas and
principles I had learned in Italy for a year and a half until a meeting with Steve Hanson, the
dynamic head of B.R. Guest Restaurants, changed my career path. By December 2000 I was
setting up Fiamma. The restaurant's name means "flame" in Italian, and I think of it as
symbolizing the passion that my time abroad ignited in me.

This book is the result of those experiences and how I have interpreted them in an American
setting. I have been greatly aided by the talented
chefs and staff I work with every day. I am
indebted to our very talented pastry chef Elizabeth
Katz. Although also not Italian by heritage, she
has mastered and embraced some of the great
classics as well as the spirit of what Italian *dolci*
should be.

As you prepare and eat the dishes in this book,
I hope you will taste my passion for contemporary
Italian cuisine.

—Michael White
July 2006

Most great Italian chefs grow up with a mother or *nonna*

in the kitchen to teach them how to make perfect pasta and *ragù*. Or they enter restaurants at a low level and work their way up over the years. Having discovered my passion for Italian cooking relatively late—I was already nineteen years old and of Norwegian heritage—I felt that the only way to truly understand the cuisine was to go to Italy and learn from the ground up about the ingredients, techniques, and traditions on which it was built.

By the time I returned to America seven years later, I had eaten and cooked in some of Italy's finest restaurants. Translating the knowledge and experience I gained into a highly praised restaurant in America that serves contemporary Italian food is the basis for this book; Fiamma is that restaurant.

INGREDIENTS FIRST

When I arrived in Bologna at the end of 1993, I knew only two Italian words: *ciao* and *cappuccino*. As I ate my way through countless small trattorias, walked through the markets, and began working in restaurants, my Italian vocabulary quickly grew. Each time I encountered an unfamiliar ingredient, and there were many—like the *puntarelle* (chicory) I saw in Rome's Piazza del Campo market—I made a note of it. Over time, I came to know the Italian names for most foods and observed how they could be used in traditional and contemporary dishes.

While I was already familiar with certain ingredients regularly used for Italian-style cooking in America, once there I frequently found that they tasted much better in Italy. For example, the prosciutto I cooked with while attending culinary school in Chicago was either a Canadian or American version of the famous cured ham from Parma. Real San Daniele prosciutto was still unavailable to Americans. When I finally sampled the original, it was a revelation.

Today, prosciutto and other cured meats, like speck, mortadella, and certain types of *salumi*, are being imported. I serve silky, paper-thin slices of it with fruit and use it to flavor sauces, vegetables, and pastas like Gemelli with Asparagus (page 74).

Beyond large *carciofi* (artichokes) that were steamed, boiled, or fried in the style of the old Jewish ghetto, I discovered small purple-tinged ones with no choke at all. They are so tender that cooks shave them into transparent slices and toss them raw in salads. Today, artichokes figure in many of my dishes; they are combined with sea scallops and black truffles in an antipasto, tossed with pasta, made into caponata, and braised with fennel and served as the base for John Dory fillets. (Because artichokes really are best when freshly cooked, directions on how to prepare them are on page 69.)

Whenever I encountered fruits, like the tree-ripened peaches of Castel del Rio in Emilia-Romagna, they were almost always picked and eaten at their peak. Or they were made into preserves. Just thinking about the luscious aroma that perfumes the air in that small hill town from late spring through summer makes my mouth water.

Traditionally, Italians add peaches to sweetened red wine, oven-roast them, and use them in simple tarts. They also make peach ice tea with them. Some chefs also use them in savory dishes. In that spirit, I oven-roast peach halves that are glazed with bitter-sweet chestnut honey, another specialty from Castel del Rio, as a tasty complement to pork roast (page 154).

Other Italian staples, like treviso, also known as *radicchio rosso di Treviso,* I had never seen. Upon tasting it, however, I quickly learned to appreciate the leafy red vegetable's slightly bitter taste in salads. It was also delicious when cut into wedges and grilled.

Like many chefs before me, I was discovering that quality ingredients are the essential foundation of Italy's good food. The beauty of cooking at restaurants like the two-starred San Domenico in Imola is that even the most basic components for chicken stock were exceptional. They tasted like

those foods really should taste. When you chop celery, the air is filled with the intensely earthy, savory aroma of that vegetable as it comes from the ground. Onions have a potent bite that can be tamed into caramel sweetness with slow sautéing, and carrots are incredibly sweet and tender.

Although foods from around the globe are available to many chefs today, most Italians don't feel a need to incorporate each newly imported herb or vegetable. First and foremost, San Domenico is built on tradition, and there is little desire on the part of their chefs to change.

That is not to say that nothing new is ever used in contemporary Italian kitchens. Where would Italy be without that sixteenth-century New World gift, the tomato? And luxury items like caviar and foie gras are expected by well-traveled guests. To add an Italian touch to the seared French duck liver served at San Domenico, the pan is deglazed with Vin Santo, a fortified sweet wine, and the liver is served with sautéed peaches.

There is also a lot of salmon available around the world. While not indigenous to Italy, the fish is now being imported and gaining popularity among locals.

TECHNIQUES

Just as Italian chefs are fastidious about their choice of ingredients, they also place great emphasis on simple preparations that respect the taste and texture of foods. Fish is rarely masked with sauces or fancy garnishes. In little trattorias along the Adriatic, most fish is simply grilled—usually on the bone—and served with a simple condiment like *Salmoriglio* sauce (page 109), an herb-scented vinaigrette. Or it is poached in *acqua pazza,* a pot of water with garlic, chiles, and tomatoes with a few aromatics added. (Our slightly more elaborate version is on page 107.) With only a few ingredients in most dishes, chefs carefully coax out every nuance of flavor from each.

Some restaurants still use centuries-old techniques to prepare foods that are remarkably tasty and satisfying to modern palates. Cooking foods in "tonno," or gently braising them in oil, is a method of preserving foods used by early Ligurian fishermen long before refrigeration. The term refers to their technique of preserving fresh-caught tuna, or *tonno,* that they used to trade with their Piemontese neighbors to the north.

The Piemontese used this same method to preserve local rabbits and ducks. For Tonno di Coniglio (page 151), the rabbit is slowly braised in oil and becomes tender and infused with the savory flavors of herbs, vegetables, and earthy porcini mushrooms.

Even in the most contemporary kitchens in Italy, vegetables are well cooked. They are boiled, sautéed, or steamed until really tender, not crisp. This enhances the taste and texture of bitter greens, like rapini, that need time to tame their bite.

Working alongside highly respected chefs like Valentino Marcattilii of San Domenico, and even people who briefly touched my life, such as the butcher who showed me how to break down animal carcasses correctly while I was working in the meat market one afternoon, taught me many valuable lessons. All of these experiences helped me gain a solid understanding of Italian cooking, both from a classical perspective and how it is evolving.

MAKING A TRANSITION

After I returned to America, plans for Osteria Fiamma started to fall into place. Soon, however, I found many of the ingredients available to me in New York were not like their Italian counterparts. The wheat used for flour is different, the varieties of fish are not the same, nor are many cuts of meat. Some Italian foods don't exist here at all.

Instead of bemoaning what is unattainable from Italy, I became determined to showcase the best of what is available from local farmers, markets, specialty food stores, and the Internet, and use those ingredients— along with a few irreplaceable imported ingredients like *Saba* (page 118) or *Mostarda* (page 263)—in an Italian manner. By now I had come to describe my cooking as inspired by the ingredients and techniques used by the finest chefs in Italy today as applied to our culinary landscape.

But America is a huge country that isn't homogeneous.

It was a liberating moment for me when I realized that no matter where you are cooking in America—be it at Fiamma in Scottsdale, Las Vegas, or New York—a dish's success starts with selecting each ingredient at its peak. This means that you or my chefs may need to substitute a locally grown vegetable or fish that, while different from what is used in New York, will be better because it is fresher.

All ingredients should be prepared with care, so that when they are cooked you can still appreciate their unique taste and texture. In a dish as simple as *bruschetta,* using local vine-ripened or heirloom tomatoes, rather than the off-season tomatoes sold in most supermarkets, can make it dramatically better.

Understanding Italian cooking methods, ways of combining ingredients, and familiar presentations have allowed me to create modern dishes that have a sensible foundation. It allows me to build intelligently upon them in the kitchen. For example, even though meaty, rectangular-cut short ribs are not found in Italy, by braising them in the Italian style, this tough cut of meat becomes fork tender and tasty.

My goal remains to capture rich, real flavors in simple, satisfying meals without artifice or camouflage. The food should be the star of the meal. My dishes are plated in an uncomplicated fashion and, when garnished, this last detail always relates to the other ingredients in the dish.

I believe that "less is more." Choose a few of the finest ingredients, simplify the preparation, and the true quality of each component will shine through. This is seen in a dish like Pasta Quills with San Daniele Prosciutto, Spring Peas, and Cream (page 72). As you taste it, everything has a value both visually and on your tongue: the al dente ridged pasta quills are balanced by the slightly firm, salty ham, nutty Parmigiano-Reggiano cheese, creamy truffle sauce, and sweet green peas.

COOKING FROM THIS BOOK

As you read through this book, some of these recipes may look complicated. But even those with multiple components are organized in a logical order to simplify the preparation.

I walk you through the recipes in a way that will help you understand how—and often more importantly, why—I do things a certain way. If I suggest cooking fish whole, for example, it is because experience has taught me that the bones and skin keep the meat juicier. This not only helps you to succeed with the dishes in this book; but hopefully it will also expand your cooking knowledge for use in other recipes.

Time and again you will read in my recipes, "When browning meat in fat, you should hear the pieces sizzle as they are added," because only when the oil is very hot will it seal the surface and lock in the juices that keep the dish moist and flavorful. Making good food is about using all of your senses.

Smell and taste also play a role. The first whiff of a dish whets your appetite even before you take a bite. But dishes should be tasted before serving them. An additional sprinkle of salt or a final drizzle of lemon-flavored olive oil are little details that can really enhance the whole dish.

Because no two people cook or perceive taste exactly the same way, I suggest you use these recipes as a guide to my thinking about how a dish should be prepared and seasoned. But eating is about pleasing your palate. After you make a recipe once or twice, you own it. Feel free to change it to suit your style or needs.

If you don't like the halibut in the recipe with couscous (page 115), or you can't find the fish in your market, substitute another 1-inch-thick, firm white fish fillet. If couscous is not to your liking, try orzo or even rice. Similarly, beef or chicken can be stand-ins for venison and game birds.

If you want to adjust the level of acid in a dish, an extra squeeze of lemon juice or a few drops of balsamic vinegar can achieve that. As for oil, I adore great olive oil; it adds immeasurably to many dishes, be it as a medium in which to cook foods, as a dressing, or as a final garnish. You can reduce the amount of oil in these recipes, if you prefer. But if you cut out too much, you risk removing not only the taste but the mouth feel and attractive sheen as well.

Throughout this book I have shared some of the experiences that flavored my culinary education in Italy. As you read about them, I hope they help you to become comfortable with the ingredients and techniques that I use. Where appropriate, I have suggested substitutions for certain foods. But, as I said earlier, some imported ingredients are so unique and impart such a distinct flavor or texture that I hope you will seek them out. Fortunately, they are becoming more readily available. At the end of the book is a list of some suggested sources.

One of the most valuable lessons I learned in Italy was to enjoy a meal in its entirety. While good food is important, so is sitting down and relaxing with friends and family. At its best, a meal can be a lengthy interlude built around several well-prepared dishes and seasoned with stimulating conversation. But even a simple two-course meal can be a special celebration.

If there is magic in my food, as some people have described it, I think it comes from the profound pleasure achieved when fine ingredients are put together in a respectful—albeit simple and modern—way so that they are recognizable and taste like what they are. For me, this is the essence of contemporary Italian cooking in America.

antipasti

Insalata di Misticanza Bibb Lettuce and Arugula Salad with Grape Tomatoes, Robiola Crostino, and White Balsamic Vinegar Insalata di Finocchio, Rucola e Nocciole Fennel, Arugula, and Hazelnut Salad Puntarelle con Salsa alle Acciughe Chicory Salad with Anchovy Vinaigrette Insalata di Barbabietole Arrosto Roasted Beets with Shaved Parmigiano and Hazelnut Vinaigrette Insalata Tiepida di Asparagi Warm Asparagus Salad Insalata di Polpo Grilled Octopus Salad Fiori di Zucchine Ripiene con Salsa Fresca di Pomodori Fried Zucchini Flowers with Fresh Tomato Sauce Scamorza Fritta con Salsa Verde Fried Scamorza Cheese with Green Sauce Capesante con Carciofi Fritti e Salsa di Tartufi Sautéed Sea Scallops, Crispy Artichokes, and Truffle Vinaigrette Gamberi Affogati in Olio d'Oliva con Carciofi Olive Oil Poached Shrimp with Artichokes Gamberi con Fagioli Giganti Shrimp with Gigante Beans Triglie con Patate e Puntarelle Red Mullet, Potato, and Baby Chicory Salad Brodetto di Vongole Clams in Simple Broth Zuppa di Zucca Arrosto con Noci, Cavolini e Funghi Roasted Pumpkin Soup with Toasted Walnuts, Brussels Sprouts, and Black Trumpet Mushrooms La Mia Zuppa Toscana di Fagioli, Cavolo Nero e Farro My Tuscan Bean Soup with Kale and Spelt Zuppa di Lenticchie Lentil Soup Cacio e Ovo Soup of Bitter Greens with Cheese Dumplings Crema di Carciofi e Topinambur Creamy Artichoke and Sunchoke Soup Carne all'Albese Minced Tenderloin of Beef with White Truffles

ANTIPASTI

When speaking of dining in Italy, the word "antipasto" is used two ways. First, it refers to the prelude to a meal when diners typically enjoy a few savory little bites, or *assagini*, with a glass of wine or San Pellegrino and bitters to tease the appetite. These can be as simple as a few olives and pieces of Parmigiano-Reggiano or *affettato*—thin slices of salami—on a small plate. A larger antipasto might include an assortment of pickled or marinated vegetables, several kinds of sausages or meats, and cheeses.

At the table, the small course preceding either the pasta or entrée is also called an antipasto. In both cases, the antipasto is meant to excite the taste buds rather than diminish the appetite. With more substantial food to follow, diners eat with restraint.

At Fiamma, some of our antipasti are classics. Soup of bitter greens with cheese dumplings has been made in Abruzzo for generations. Throughout Italy, when vine-ripened tomatoes are available, there is a good chance that bruschetta will be served. Other antipasti, like artichokes and shrimp poached in olive oil and fried *scamorza* cheese with *salsa verde*, or green sauce, are more contemporary but based on traditional preparations.

Many are determined by the seasons. You won't find *fior di zucchine fritti* on our menu until summer. But when they are available, you will remember those deliciously crunchy, lightly battered, stuffed zucchini flowers with fresh tomato sauce with pleasure. Roasted beets with shaved Parmigiano-Reggiano and toasted hazelnuts showered on top are more typical in the spring and fall.

Italians are also passionate about soups. Depending on the time of year, our menu might include Roasted Pumpkin Soup with Toasted Walnuts, Brussels Sprouts, and Black Trumpet Mushrooms, or Creamy Artichoke and Sunchoke Soup. This chapter also includes my robust version of Tuscan Bean Soup with Kale and Spelt.

Because Americans love salads in almost any guise—and far more so than Italians— I include a variety of greens and vegetables combined with shellfish, game meats, and legumes. They range from Fennel, Arugula, and Hazelnut Salad to Grilled Octopus Salad (one of the restaurant's most popular dishes). All of our salads are dressed with vinaigrettes that are light in character but assertive in flavor and as varied as one scented with anchovies, another with hazelnuts, and still another with fresh mint. Anyone stuck in the "mixed field greens tossed with balsamic vinegar and olive oil" mode will find them a wake-up call to some exciting possibilities.

The antipasti in this chapter have been among the most popular dishes on our menu since the restaurant opened. All are easy to make at home. Savor them before lunch or dinner. Or, while it is decidedly untraditional in Italy, here in America you might enjoy several of these dishes as a light supper. That certainly is the case for me with those creamy squares of Fried Scamorza Cheese with Green Sauce.

I also suggest being a little gutsy with your appetizers. Because they are not the entire meal, you might experiment: take a component from one recipe in this chapter, such as the vinaigrette, and combine it with other salad ingredients to make your own personal creation. That's what we do in my kitchen. It is how some great dishes evolve.

Insalata di Misticanza
Bibb Lettuce and Arugula Salad with Grape Tomatoes, Robiola Crostino, and White Balsamic Vinegar

[MAKES 4 SERVINGS]

Italian chefs and home gardeners select lettuces with different tastes, textures, and colors according to the best available that day, so each salad is unique in character. Use my choices as a guide, and feel free to change them. The thin toast, or *crostino*, topped with creamy, tangy *robiola* cheese from Piemonte, is a pleasing foil for this salad tossed with white balsamic vinaigrette. I also like that the white balsamic vinegar dresses salads without camouflaging the colors. It has a slightly sharper taste than the familiar dark, sweet *balsamico*. If unavailable, use conventional balsamic vinegar.

½ small bulb fennel, trimmed

1 head Bibb or Boston lettuce, washed and dried, with coarse stems discarded, and torn into bite-size pieces

1 small head radicchio, washed, dried, and torn into bite-size pieces

Leaves from 1 small bunch baby arugula, washed and dried

½ small seedless cucumber, peeled and diced

1 cup grape tomatoes, cut in half

1 small bunch radishes, trimmed and thinly sliced

4 ounces (½ cup) fresh robiola cheese or ¼ cup each whole milk ricotta and goat cheese

2 tablespoons minced fresh chives

½ cup plus 2 tablespoons extra-virgin olive oil

continued

4 thin slices baguette or other narrow loaf, lightly toasted

3 tablespoons balsamic vinegar, preferably white

Sea salt and freshly ground black pepper

¼ cup salted or unsalted sunflower seeds, toasted (see page 171)

Remove and discard the outside layer of the fennel and remove the core. Using a mandoline or very sharp knife, cut the fennel crosswise into very thin slices and put them into a large salad bowl. Add the lettuce, radicchio, arugula, cucumber, tomato, and radish and toss.

Using a wooden spoon, mash together the robiola cheese, chives, and the 2 tablespoons of the olive oil in a bowl until smooth. Spread on the *crostini*.

In another bowl, whisk together the ½ cup olive oil and the vinegar, season to taste with salt and pepper, drizzle over the salad, and toss. Divide the salad among 4 plates, add a *crostino* atop each, and sprinkle with sunflower seeds. Serve at once.

Arugula

Baby arugula leaves are very tender and don't need to have the stems trimmed. Some supermarkets sell them loose or in plastic bags. If arugula is bought in bunches, store it in a plastic bag with a damp paper towel wrapped around the stems; trim coarse stems, and wash it just before using. It will keep for up to a week.

Insalata di Finocchio, Rucola e Nocciole
Fennel, Arugula, and Hazelnut Salad

Sometimes we simply want an appealing, light salad to enjoy as a light first course or side dish. This combination will fill that desire.

1 large bulb fennel

½ medium red onion

2 cups lightly packed, washed, and dried arugula leaves

3 to 4 tablespoons hazelnut oil or extra-virgin olive oil,
   plus extra for drizzling

2 tablespoons freshly squeezed lemon juice

Sea salt and freshly ground black pepper

1 small piece Parmigiano-Reggiano cheese (about 2 ounces), for shaving

½ cup coarsely cracked, toasted hazelnuts (see page 116), for garnish

Remove and discard the outside layer of the fennel. Reserve the fronds. Cut the bulb in half lengthwise and remove the core. Using a mandoline or very sharp knife, cut the fennel crosswise into very thin slices and put them into a large bowl. Cut the red onion crosswise into very thin slices and add them to the bowl. Add the arugula, hazelnut oil, and lemon juice and toss to blend. Season to taste with salt and pepper and toss again.

Spoon the salad onto a large platter. Using a vegetable peeler, shave thin slices of Parmigiano-Reggiano over the salad. Drizzle on a little more oil and add some black pepper. Coarsely chop about a tablespoon of the reserved fennel fronds, sprinkle them and the hazelnuts on the salad, and serve.

Puntarelle con Salsa alle Acciughe
Chicory Salad with Anchovy Vinaigrette

[MAKES 4 SERVINGS]

This simple salad is like those you commonly find in Roman trattorias from Trastevere to the Jewish Ghetto. Served either as an appetizer or *contorno,* a side dish, it is like a Caesar salad personified but made with sharper—you might say "barnyardy"—tasting Pecorino Romano cheese rather than familiar Parmigiano-Reggiano. I think the sheep's milk cheese stands up better to the assertive greens. The salad's salty, mildly bitter tastes make an excellent partner for juicy Roast Chicken (page 140) and Rosemary Roasted Potatoes (page 193).

Puntarelle are crisp, somewhat sharp-tasting stalks of chicory. Once trimmed and cut up, the stalks should soak in cold water for about 30 minutes to keep them crisp, but they can stay in water for several hours. When ready to serve *puntarelle,* dry the pieces in a salad spinner.

One 2-ounce tin anchovies packed in salt, rinsed and
   patted dry with paper towels

2 large egg yolks

2 tablespoons capers, drained

Juice of 2 lemons

2 tablespoons white wine vinegar

⅔ cup extra-virgin olive oil

8 cups baby chicory, washed, dried, and cut into
   bite-size pieces (see headnote)

1 cup toasted bread croutons (see sidebar)

¼ cup freshly grated Pecorino Romano cheese

Sea salt and freshly ground black pepper

Red pepper flakes to taste

Combine the anchovies, egg yolks, capers, lemon juice, and vinegar in an electric blender and purée until smooth. Stop the machine, scrape down the sides, add the olive oil, and blend until the ingredients are emulsified and completely smooth. Set aside. (This may be done by hand, in which case, you should mash the anchovies before blending, then add all of the ingredients before the olive oil, and whisk in the oil in a slow steady stream.)

In a large bowl, toss the *puntarelle* and croutons with the vinaigrette. Sprinkle on the Pecorino cheese, toss again, season to taste with salt, pepper, and pepper flakes and serve.

Mollica

My favorite way of making great croutons is to reach inside a loaf of Italian white bread and pull out the *mollica*, or soft part, and tear it into irregular, 1-inch pieces. I toss them with a little fragrant olive oil and bake them in a preheated 400°F oven until golden brown, about 5 minutes, shaking the pan occasionally, then season them with salt before serving.

Insalata di Barbabietole Arrosto
Roasted Beets with Shaved Parmigiano and Hazelnut Vinaigrette

[MAKES 4 SERVINGS]

Many local farmstands and markets sell different varieties and colors of beets, some with unique markings. The beauty of this salad is the colorful combination of candy cane, yellow, and red beets, but any beets may be used. Roasting the unpeeled beets over salt intensifies their flavor and makes them sweeter.

Coarse rock salt

1 pound mixed beets, each about 2 inches in diameter, stems and roots trimmed

¼ cup hazelnut oil

2 tablespoons balsamic vinegar

½ cup Pecorino Romano cheese, preferably with black truffles, cut into ½-inch cubes

Sea salt and coarsely ground black pepper

2 cups mâche, watercress, or arugula, washed and dried, coarse stems removed, and leaves torn into bite-size pieces

¼ cup coarsely chopped, toasted hazelnuts (see page 116)

Preheat the oven to 375°F. Cover the bottom of a jelly-roll pan with rock salt. Place the beets on top of the salt and roast until very tender when pierced with the tip of a knife; begin testing after about 1 hour. Remove the pan from the oven and let the beets cool completely. When cool, put them in a clean, old towel and rub to remove the skin.

Cut the beets into ¼-inch cubes and put them in a large bowl. Stir the hazelnut oil and balsamic vinegar together in a small bowl, pour over the beets, and toss to blend. Add the Pecorino cheese, season to taste with salt and pepper, and toss again.

Divide the mâche among 4 salad plates. Spoon on the beet-cheese mixture, add a pinch of salt and pepper, sprinkle on the hazelnuts, and serve.

Insalata Tiepida di Asparagi
Warm Asparagus Salad

Asparagus and morels arrive together as harbingers of spring and make splendid partners in this warm salad. When I was growing up in Wisconsin, morels were easy to find in the woods near where we lived and not considered a luxury. I know we were in the minority, even among the chefs in those days. All varieties of wild mushrooms are more readily available today in specialty food stores, on the Internet, and many supermarkets. In this salad, fresh cremini or porcini mushrooms or rehydrated dried morels may be substituted. Black summer Italian truffle juice, available from several specialty food suppliers, is a relatively inexpensive way of adding the uniquely luxurious flavor that only truffles can give to a dish.

1 pound medium to thick asparagus with the bottoms snapped off, peeled

½ pound morel mushrooms, rinsed, stems trimmed, and patted dry with paper towels

½ cup extra-virgin olive oil

1 shallot, minced

2 tablespoons freshly squeezed lemon juice

¼ cup black truffle juice (optional, see Sources, page 266)

2 teaspoons Dijon mustard

Coarse sea salt

Freshly ground black pepper

1 bunch frisée with dark outer dark green leaves and coarse parts of the stems removed, washed and dried, and separated into leaves

¼ pound Parmigiano-Reggiano cheese, shaved

Cook the asparagus in boiling salted water until crisp-tender, 5 to 8 minutes, depending on the thickness. Drain, shock under cold water, then blot dry with paper towels. Cut the asparagus on the diagonal into 1½-inch pieces and reserve.

Halve the large morels. Heat 4 tablespoons of olive oil in a large saucepan over medium heat. Add the mushrooms and cook, stirring occasionally, for 3 to 4 minutes, until they start to soften.

Add the shallot and continue cooking, stirring occasionally, until it is translucent, about 2 minutes. Remove from the heat and set aside.

In a small bowl, combine the lemon juice, truffle juice, mustard, and about a teaspoon of salt. Slowly whisk in the remaining 4 tablespoons of olive oil until emulsified. Combine the asparagus and mushrooms in a large bowl and toss gently with all but 1 tablespoon of the vinaigrette. Season liberally with black pepper.

Line a large plate with the frisée and spoon on the asparagus salad. Top with the shaved Parmigiano and drizzle on the remaining vinaigrette before serving.

Insalata di Polpo
Grilled Octopus Salad

[MAKES 4 SERVINGS]

I can easily imagine myself in a little
Adriatic seaside village eating this simple, tasty salad. Italians love grilled foods,
and the smell of this octopus is so fragrant it makes my mouth water in anticipation. Once grilled,
the sliced octopus—with little caramelized spots on the surface—is tossed with
meaty, green Cerignola olives from Puglia, radicchio, and endive in a minty vinaigrette.
To keep octopus tender, start cooking it in cold water with a little acid, like red wine, added and gently
simmer it until barely done. If dropped into boiling liquid, the legs curl up and it becomes tough.
Slicing octopus after cooking also helps keep the pieces tender and moist. An Italian myth says if you
put a couple of corks in the liquid, it prevents octopus from getting tough.
Follow my method, and you won't have that problem.

Octopus

1 pound cleaned octopus with heads removed (1½ to 1¾ pounds uncleaned)

2 cups full-bodied red wine, such as Chianti or Sangiovese

1 small yellow onion, finely chopped

1 small carrot, peeled and finely chopped

1 small rib celery, trimmed and finely chopped

2 sprigs fresh thyme

1 bay leaf

4 cloves garlic, crushed

3 tablespoons extra-virgin olive oil

Juice of 1 lime

continued

14

Salad

> ¾ cup extra-virgin olive oil
>
> ½ cup red wine vinegar
>
> Juice of 2 limes
>
> 1 bunch fresh mint, stems removed and leaves torn into pieces
>
> ½ cup chopped green olives, preferably Cerignola
>   (available at specialty olive bars)
>
> Sea salt and freshly ground black pepper
>
> 2 endives, cored and julienned
>
> 1 small head radicchio, washed and dried, cored and julienned
>
> 2 cups cooked chickpeas or gigante beans (see sidebar)

To cook the Octopus:

Place the octopus in a pot with the wine and enough cold water to cover. Add the onion, carrot, celery, thyme, and bay leaf; bring to a gentle simmer over medium heat and cook until opaque, 20 to 30 minutes. Remove the octopus with a slotted spoon and set aside to cool. (The octopus may be cooked a day ahead and refrigerated in a covered bowl.)

Transfer the octopus to a resealable plastic bag, add the garlic, olive oil, and lime juice; seal and refrigerate for 2 hours, then remove the octopus from the marinade and set aside.

Preheat a charcoal or gas grill until hot. Position the rack 5 to 6 inches from the heat.

For the Salad:

Combine the olive oil, vinegar, lime juice, mint leaves, and green olives in the jar of an electric blender and purée into a smooth emulsion. Or whisk them together in a small bowl. (If done this way, the texture will be less smooth.) Season to taste with salt and pepper and set aside.

Toss the endives, radicchio, and chickpeas together in a salad bowl.

Grill the octopus for 4 to 5 minutes, turning once after 2 to 3 minutes, until the pieces are browned in spots and nicely caramelized but not burned. Remove, toss with the greens and vinaigrette, divide among 4 plates, and serve.

Dried versus Canned Chickpeas

In many recipes, rather than soaking and boiling dried chickpeas, you can use rinsed and drained canned chickpeas or jarred gigante beans, available at some Italian grocery stores. While they work fine, those you cook yourself will be tastier and have a better, less mushy texture.

There are two methods of soaking beans. The traditional way is to put them in a large pot of cold water overnight, then discard the water before cooking the beans. (To cook, bring to a boil in a fresh pot of water, and cook until tender, about an hour.)

For the second or "quick" soaking method, put the beans in a pot with enough cold water to cover. Cover the pot and bring the water to a boil. Cook for 2 minutes, turn off the heat, and let them stand for 1 hour. (Then cook in a fresh pot of water as instructed above.) Both soaking methods work well. Very old beans may require longer cooking to become tender.

Fiori di Zucchine Ripiene con Salsa Fresca di Pomodori
Fried Zucchini Flowers with Fresh Tomato Sauce

[MAKES 6 SERVINGS]

Fried zucchini flowers served with fresh tomato sauce is one of our most popular seasonal dishes. The delicate blossoms filled with mozzarella and anchovies are fried until golden and crispy. The uncooked sauce is made with fresh ripe tomatoes.

Fresh Tomato Sauce

2 large ripe tomatoes, peeled (see page 105), seeded, and chopped (about 1½ cups)

2 tablespoons finely chopped red onion

1 tablespoon extra-virgin olive oil

½ small clove garlic

2 to 3 fresh basil leaves, torn into large pieces, plus extra leaves, for garnish

1 to 2 teaspoons red wine vinegar

Sea salt and freshly ground black pepper

Fried Zucchini

1 cup all-purpose flour

6 ounces fresh mozzarella, cut into twelve ¼-inch-thick slices

12 oil-packed anchovy fillets, rinsed and patted with paper towels

12 zucchini flowers, trimmed with 2 inches of stem left intact, pistils removed, gently washed, and patted dry

1 large egg, beaten

¼ cup ice water

Olive oil, for frying

For the Fresh Tomato Sauce:

Combine the tomatoes, onion, olive oil, and garlic in a food processor and pulse until almost smooth. Stir in the basil, then season to taste with vinegar, salt, and pepper. Set aside.

To make the Fried Zucchini:

Put the flour into a wide, shallow bowl. Carefully place a piece of mozzarella and an anchovy inside each zucchini flower, twist the petals together like a twist-tie, and lightly dust the flowers with flour, shaking off the excess.

In a deep mixing bowl, beat the egg and ice water until blended. Whisk in about 3 tablespoons of the flour and mix until the batter is the consistency of heavy cream.

Pour 3 inches oil into a deep-fryer or large, heavy pot and heat to 375°F. Holding the zucchini flowers by the stem, dip 2 flowers at a time into the batter to coat completely, letting the excess drip off.

Add the flowers to the hot oil and fry until crisp and golden brown, about 2 minutes. Remove and drain on a platter lined with paper towels. While still hot, season them with salt and a little pepper to taste. Repeat with the remaining zucchini flowers. Serve hot with a little fresh tomato sauce drizzled on top and a basil leaf to garnish.

Scamorza Fritta con Salsa Verde
Fried Scamorza Cheese with Green Sauce

For this savory appetizer or entrée, I use *scamorza* cheese, a mild tasting, aged mozzarella with a denser texture than the fresh form. Although balls of *scamorza* have a crust, the cheese inside remains soft. The cheese is sometimes smoked over wood chips, adding a smoky taste and darkened exterior.

2 cups lightly packed fresh basil leaves

½ cup packed fresh flat-leaf parsley leaves

¼ cup packed fresh mint leaves

4 oil-packed anchovy fillets, rinsed and patted with paper towels

2 tablespoons freshly grated Pecorino Romano cheese

1 tablespoon capers, drained

½ cup plus 1 tablespoon extra-virgin olive oil

Sea salt and freshly ground pepper

¼ cup all-purpose flour

Four ⅓-inch-thick slices scamorza cheese (1½ to 2 ounces each)

4 thick slices rustic bread, toasted

In a food processor, combine the basil, parsley, mint, anchovies, Pecorino, and capers; pulse until finely chopped. With the machine running, add the ½ cup of olive oil in a slow, steady stream and process until smooth. Season to taste with salt and pepper.

Spread the flour in a flat bowl. Lightly dredge the cheese slices with flour, patting to remove the excess. In a medium nonstick skillet, heat the 1 tablespoon olive oil over medium heat. Add the cheese and fry, turning once, until golden, 3 to 4 minutes total cooking time. Transfer the cheese to 4 plates, drizzle on the sauce, and serve with the toasted bread alongside.

Capesante con Carciofi Fritti e Salsa di Tartufi
Sautéed Sea Scallops, Crispy Artichokes, and Truffle Vinaigrette

[MAKES 4 SERVINGS]

I like to marry old dishes with contemporary ingredients. For this tasty dish, crispy, twice-cooked *carciofi alla giudia*—the classic Jewish-style artichokes from the Roman ghetto—and succulent diver or large sea scallops are complemented by slightly bitter tasting, slender green frisée leaves. White truffle oil and balsamic vinegar seal the match. As the scallops cook, they are basted with nutty-brown rosemary butter. It adds a lush, herbaceous flavor to this fragrant dish. Searing the shellfish over medium-high heat rather than a high blast of fire keeps them juicier. At better markets, ask for "dry" scallops: those that have not been soaked in water and/or treated with chemicals to make them plumper. "Wet" scallops lose a lot of moisture during cooking.

9 tablespoons extra-virgin olive oil

2 tablespoons white truffle oil (see Sources, page 266)

2 tablespoons balsamic vinegar

Sea salt and freshly ground black pepper

1 pound baby artichokes, outer leaves removed, stems peeled and quartered (see page 24), or substitute one 9-ounce package frozen baby artichokes, defrosted and blotted dry with paper towels and quartered, if not cut

12 large sea scallops, with tendon removed, blotted dry

1 tablespoon unsalted butter

1 sprig fresh rosemary

1 head frisée with coarse stems removed, washed, dried, and broken into bite-size pieces (about 2 cups)

In a small bowl, whisk together 4 tablespoons of the olive oil, the truffle oil, and balsamic vinegar. Season to taste with salt and pepper and set aside.

Heat another 4 tablespoons of the olive oil in a deep skillet over medium heat until hot. Add the artichokes and cook gently until tender, 12 to 15 minutes. (If using frozen artichokes, this will take about 5 minutes less time.) Remove the artichokes with a slotted spoon and transfer to a sheet pan to cool.

Turn the oven to warm. Reheat the oil over high heat until hot. Return the artichokes to the oil and cook until crispy and golden brown, about 5 minutes. Remove and drain on paper towels. Put them on the sheet pan and transfer to the oven to keep warm.

Season the scallops with salt and pepper. Heat a large skillet, preferably cast iron, over medium-high heat until hot. Add the remaining tablespoon of olive oil, then the scallops, and cook without moving until they are richly browned on one side, about 2 minutes. Turn, add the butter and rosemary sprig, and cook for 2 minutes longer, basting frequently with the butter until the scallops are richly browned on the second side.

Divide the frisée among 4 salad plates. Spoon on the artichokes and top with the scallops. Drizzle with the truffle vinaigrette and serve.

Carciofi alla Giudia (Artichokes in the Jewish-style)

In the United States, large, round globe artichokes are available all year long; in Italy there are two distinct seasons. In spring you find the prized, purple-tinged Roman artichokes which, when small, are very tender and have no chokes. Yearly festivals in Rome celebrate the many ways they can be served. One of the most beloved classics is *carciofi alla giudia*, artichokes in the Jewish style.

To prepare them, pull off the tough outer leaves and peel the long stems with a potato peeler. If you can't find baby artichokes, use the smallest ones you can find and trim out the fuzzy choke. Rub them with lemon juice or put them in a bowl of acidulated water (water with a few drops of lemon juice added) and let them stand while cleaning the remaining artichokes. Remove the artichokes and turn them upside down on paper towels to dry. Fill a deep pot about halfway with oil and heat over medium heat. Add the artichokes and simmer until the heart is tender and can be pierced with the tip of a knife. Remove and cool. Heat the oil again and when hot, add the artichokes and deep-fry them until crisp, turning often. Serve hot or let them cool to room temperature and season them with a few drops of lemon juice and a little salt.

Gamberi Affogati in Olio d'Oliva con Carciofi
Olive Oil Poached Shrimp with Artichokes

[MAKES 4 SERVINGS]

Rosy jumbo shrimp and pale green artichoke hearts are joined in a simple vinaigrette that uses the same olive oil in which the shellfish were gently poached. The pair are combined with grape tomatoes and herbs for this colorful warm weather salad. Once the artichokes are cooked (they may be done ahead), the salad is quickly finished. Other vegetables such as string beans, asparagus, or diced potatoes may be substituted for the artichokes. If the dressing separates in the blender before serving, reemulsify it by adding 1 tablespoon cold water and blending again.

1 cup extra-virgin olive oil

3 cloves garlic, crushed

12 jumbo shrimp, peeled and deveined

5 cooked artichoke hearts (see page 69)

1 cup grape or cherry tomatoes, quartered

1 cup loosely packed fresh herb leaves, such as basil, flat-leaf parsley, and fresh fennel fronds

Juice of 1 lemon

Sea salt and coarsely ground black pepper

In a large deep saucepan, heat the olive oil and garlic over medium heat until warm. Add the shrimp and cook, turning occasionally, until they turn pink, about 8 minutes. Remove with a slotted spoon to a large bowl. Dice 4 artichoke hearts and combine them with the tomatoes and herbs in a separate bowl.

Remove 1/2 cup of the olive oil along with the garlic and transfer it to the jar of an electric blender. Add the remaining artichoke heart and the lemon juice and purée until smooth and emulsified. Season to taste with salt and pepper. Pour the vinaigrette over the salad, tossing to coat the ingredients evenly. Divide the salad among 4 plates. Place 3 shrimps, with their tails up, on top of each salad and serve at room temperature.

Gamberi con Fagioli Giganti
Shrimp with Gigante Beans

[MAKES 4 SERVINGS]

This simple, fresh dish is another example of how a few well-chosen ingredients can become a satisfying dining experience, especially in warm weather, when we crave lighter fare. Jumbo shrimp, gigante beans, a bulb of fennel, oranges, and arugula along with some olive oil are all that you need.

For the most succulent, flavorful shrimp buy them with the heads on, if possible. It's like cooking meat on the bone. Be careful not to overcook them, because that destroys the texture and taste.

2 tablespoons fresh rosemary leaves, minced

Juice of 3 navel oranges and freshly grated zest of 1 orange

½ cup fragrant, peppery extra-virgin olive oil

1 clove garlic, minced

12 jumbo shrimp, peeled and deveined with tails and heads still on if possible

1 medium bulb fennel

1 cup cooked gigante or cannellini beans

2 cups loosely packed arugula leaves with stems removed, rinsed and dried

2 navel oranges, segmented (see sidebar)

Sea salt and freshly ground black pepper

Lemon Olive Oil (optional; page 253), for drizzling

Combine the rosemary, the juice of 2 of the oranges, the orange zest, ¼ cup of the olive oil, the garlic, and shrimp in a large resealable plastic bag; seal and refrigerate for 2 to 4 hours.

Light a gas or charcoal grill or heat a grill pan.

Trim the fronds and base from the fennel. Cut it in half lengthwise, remove the core, and thinly slice the bulb crosswise with a mandoline or sharp knife. Combine the fennel, beans, arugula, and orange segments in a bowl. Add the remaining ¼ cup of olive oil and toss gently to blend. Add about half of

the remaining orange juice, season with salt and pepper to taste, and toss lightly. Adjust the amount of oil, orange juice, and seasonings to your taste.

Remove the shrimp from the marinade, season with salt and pepper, and place them on the hot grill. Cook until they are charred on the outside but just cooked through, about 2 minutes per side, turning once.

Divide the salad among 4 large plates. Remove the heads from the shrimp, if desired, lay 3 shrimp on the greens with the tails up, drizzle with a little Lemon Oil, and serve at once.

To Zest and Segment Oranges

Wash oranges to remove any wax or dirt. Grate the colored zest from the oranges with a zester, avoiding the white pith.

Remove the sections by cutting off a narrow slice at the top and bottom of each orange. Working over a strainer, make an incision next to the membrane of one section and another cut on the other side of the section, letting the sections fall into the strainer as they are loosened. Continue working around the orange. Once all sections are removed, squeeze the remaining juice from the orange into the bowl and reserve.

Triglie con Patate e Puntarelle
Red Mullet, Potato, and Baby Chicory Salad

[MAKES 4 SERVINGS]

Red mullet are small, firm-fleshed fish with an attractive red pattern on their skin. In this warm salad, pairs of broiled fillets lay crisscrossed over pan-fried fingerling potatoes and pale green, young chicory stems, known as *puntarelle* around Rome. The dish is drizzled with a very flavorful herb- and anchovy-infused green sauce before serving. The first time I went to Rome's large, open-air market in the Piazza del Campo, I saw dozens of vegetable sellers sitting on little stools cleaning buckets of *puntarelle*. The popular bitter green is typically cut into little squares or julienned before use. If you can't find baby chicory at local Italian markets, substitute thinly sliced American chicory, frisée, Belgian endives, or baby dandelion greens.

6 cloves garlic, thinly sliced

2 shallots, chopped

Leaves of 1 small bunch fresh thyme

½ cup extra-virgin olive oil

8 red mullet fillets with skin on or eight 2-ounce pieces
 red snapper fillet with skin on

¼ pound fingerlings or small new potatoes, peeled and cut into ½-inch slices

1 sprig fresh rosemary

Sea salt and freshly ground black pepper

1½ cups thinly sliced baby chicory (See headnote for substitutions.)

2 tablespoons freshly squeezed lemon juice

½ to ¾ cup Green Sauce (page 261)

Combine the garlic, shallots, thyme, and 2 tablespoons of the olive oil with the mullets in a large resealable plastic bag; seal and refrigerate while cooking the potatoes, or for up to 30 minutes, turning once during this time.

Heat 2 tablespoons of the olive oil in a large skillet over medium-high heat. Add the potatoes and rosemary, turn to coat with the oil, and cook until the potatoes are golden brown, 6 to 8 minutes, then turn and cook the second side until golden brown, shaking the pan occasionally, 5 to 6 minutes. Season with a liberal amount of salt and pepper, set aside, and keep warm.

In a large bowl, toss the baby chicory with the remaining ¼ cup of olive oil and the lemon juice; season to taste with salt and pepper.

Adjust the broiler rack to about 4 inches from the heat and heat the broiler. Remove the fillets from the marinade and lay them skin side down on a flat baking sheet. Broil the fillets for 4 to 5 minutes, until they are firm to the touch and the flesh looks opaque on the sides. Season generously with salt and pepper.

Add the warm potatoes to the chicory, toss, and divide among 4 plates. Top each salad with 2 fillets crossing in the center. Drizzle Green Sauce around the plates and serve at once.

Red Mullet

Around the Mediterranean, red mullet is a highly esteemed fish that is also known at goatfish. In French it is *rouget*. Look for bright red-colored flesh as the best indicator of quality. If the fish looks faded, it is past its prime. The flesh should be very firm and the skin tightly attached. As mullet is very perishable, use it within a day or two.

Brodetto di Vongole
Clams in Simple Broth

[MAKES 4 SERVINGS]

Steamed clams cooked in white wine, garlic, and leeks make a soul-satisfying meal when served with a tossed green salad, slices of crusty country bread to sop up the delectable liquid, and some wine. The fragrant simple broth, or *brodetto,* that remains in the pot once the clams are cooked is reduced, then enriched with a little butter. It is simple and easy.

When sweating leeks or other vegetables (cooking them gently in a covered pan without browning in a little fat), adding a pinch of salt to the pot helps to create moisture to soften them with a minimum of liquid. It also intensifies their taste.

¼ cup olive oil

2 cloves garlic, cut in half

Pinch of red pepper flakes

2 leeks, cleaned and light green parts thinly sliced

Sea salt

2 pounds Manila clams, scrubbed and purged (see page 122), or substitute littleneck or cherrystones

2 cups dry white wine, such as Pinot Grigio or Sauvignon Blanc

Four ½-inch-thick slices crusty baguette, lightly toasted

1 tablespoon unsalted butter

2 tablespoons chopped flat-leaf parsley

Fragrant, peppery extra-virgin olive oil, for drizzling

Heat the olive oil in a large, deep saucepan over medium heat. Add the garlic and cook until lightly colored, 1 to 2 minutes. Add the pepper flakes and cook for 30 seconds longer. Stir in the leeks and

a sprinkling of salt, cover, and sweat until soft, 1 to 2 minutes. Add the clams and wine, re-cover the pot, and steam until the clams are opened, 4 to 6 minutes. Discard any that do not open. Remove the pan from heat.

Place a slice of toast in the bottoms of 4 large, flat soup bowls and divide the clams among them.

Return the pan to the heat and reduce the liquid by half over high heat. Stir in the butter, then the parsley, and taste to adjust the seasonings. Ladle the broth over the clams, drizzle with olive oil, and serve.

Different Olive Oils for Different Reasons

Italy has many different regions, each with its own cuisines and specialty products. Many of those that I've tasted in various areas inspired my dishes. When I can find the olive oil from these regions, I try to use them in the appropriate dish.

In general, however, I prefer using lighter Ligurian oils for cooking fish. For heartier dishes, I like more intensely flavored Tuscan or Umbrian oils. In this dish, the broth is made with a reasonably priced extra-virgin olive oil. For the final drizzle, I like green oil made from the first pressing of the olives. It is unfiltered and bursting with spicy tastes. At home, choose the most flavorful olive oil you can buy to finish the dish.

Zuppa di Zucca Arrosto con Noci, Cavolini e Funghi

Roasted Pumpkin Soup with Toasted Walnuts, Brussels Sprouts, and Black Trumpet Mushrooms

[MAKES 4 SERVINGS]

The potent marriage of pumpkins, walnuts, Brussels sprouts, and trumpet mushrooms in this soup will warm your senses. It reminds me of autumn in Tuscany with colorful leaves crunching underfoot and the smell of toasted chestnuts in the air, heralding the arrival of game season. Roasting the pumpkin, rather than boiling it, concentrates the natural sugars and makes it sweeter tasting.

1 large pumpkin (about 4 pounds), cut into large chunks, seeds and fibers removed (see sidebar; about 9 cups)

4 tablespoons (½ stick) unsalted butter, melted

Sea salt and freshly ground black pepper

1 sprig fresh sage

1 bay leaf

2 tablespoons extra-virgin olive oil, plus 1 teaspoon

1 medium-large yellow onion, chopped (1 cup)

1 large rib celery, trimmed and chopped (½ cup)

1 large carrot, peeled and chopped (½ cup)

1 clove garlic, chopped

1 quart Homemade Chicken Stock (page 255) or canned low-sodium stock, heated

continued

1 cup Brussels sprouts with tough outer leaves discarded,
   trimmed and quartered

½ cup shelled walnut halves

½ cup black trumpet or other wild mushrooms, trimmed and wiped

2 teaspoons pumpkin seed oil (see Sources, page 266)

Preheat the oven to 350°F.

Toss the pumpkin with the butter and put it in a shallow baking pan, then season to taste with salt and pepper. Add the sage and bay leaf to the pan, toss once more, and bake for 45 minutes, stirring occasionally, or until the pumpkin is very soft. Scoop out the pulp and discard the rind. Discard the sage and bay leaf.

Meanwhile, heat the 2 tablespoons of oil in a large skillet over medium heat. Add the onion, celery, and carrot to the skillet. Season to taste with salt and pepper and cook, stirring often, until the onion is translucent and the carrot begins to soften, 10 to 12 minutes. Add the garlic to the skillet and cook for 2 minutes more, stirring often. Pour in ½ cup of the stock to deglaze the pan, scraping up any browned bits on the bottom, and cook for 1 minute.

Working in two batches, transfer the pumpkin and sautéed vegetables to the jar of an electric blender, add the remaining hot stock, and purée until smooth. Transfer the purée to a saucepan and reheat over low heat. Taste to adjust the seasonings and keep warm.

Bring a pot of salted water to a boil. Add the Brussels sprouts and cook for 1 minute, or just until they turn bright green. Immediately plunge them into cold water to stop the cooking, then drain.

Heat the 1 teaspoon of oil in a large, clean skillet over medium heat. Add the walnuts and toast them, stirring often, for 6 to 8 minutes until crispy. Add the mushrooms and cook, stirring, until soft, 3 minutes more. Stir in the Brussels sprouts and cook long enough to heat them through, 2 to 3 minutes. Season to taste with salt and pepper. Divide the vegetable mixture among 4 wide soup bowls. Pour in the soup, drizzle each bowl with ½ teaspoon of pumpkin seed oil, and serve.

Pumpkins in Italy

Although summer and winter squash figure in many delicious Italian dishes, they only arrived in Italy in the sixteenth century from America. I especially like cheese pumpkins, an heirloom variety grown around the New York area. Its rich orange flesh is excellent for pies and hearty soups. The tan or camel-colored pumpkin has deep ribs and a flattish shape—like a wheel of cheese—hence its name. It is also called Long Island cheese pumpkin (*curcurbita moschata*); they average between 4 and 8 pounds.

La Mia Zuppa Toscana di Fagioli, Cavolo Nero e Farro
My Tuscan Bean Soup with Kale and Spelt

Hearty Tuscan bean soup is a much loved staple that has nurtured generations, and every *nonna* has a personal recipe. For my version, I combine cranberry beans with kale and farro, or spelt, an ancient wheatlike grain believed to have nourished early Roman troops. The nutty-tasting, pale brown grain is similar to hard wheat. It has become especially popular in northern regions around Tuscany and Umbria, as well as here in America.

Cavolo nero translates as black cabbage in Italian. In America, it is known as black kale. The vegetable's transparent blue leaves are traditional in Tuscan dishes. The flavor is stronger than our kale, but either will work in this soup. It may be made ahead and reheated. If you prefer, use the short method for soaking the beans on page 17.

3 cups borlotti or cranberry beans, or substitute pinto beans

1 cup farro (spelt) or wheatberries

¼ cup extra-virgin olive oil, plus extra for drizzling

½ pound sweet Italian sausage, casings removed

1 pound kale, preferably Tuscan, coarse stems removed,
   cut into thick ribbons (about 4 cups)

1 medium-large yellow onion, diced (1 cup)

1 large carrot, peeled and diced (½ cup)

1 large rib celery, trimmed and diced (½ cup)

3 cloves garlic, thinly sliced

5 cups Homemade Chicken Stock (page 255) or canned low-sodium stock,
   plus extra if necessary

1 cup peeled (see page 105), seeded, and diced tomatoes, or substitute drained
   diced canned tomatoes

1 sprig fresh rosemary

1 sprig fresh sage

Sea salt and freshly ground black pepper

½ cup freshly grated Parmigiano-Reggiano cheese

In separate bowls, cover the beans and farro with cold water and soak overnight. Drain and carefully pick through them to remove any pebbles or foreign matter. Set aside.

In a large heavy pot, heat the olive oil over medium-high heat. Add the Italian sausage and cook, stirring occasionally, until the meat begins to separate and brown, 3 to 5 minutes, stirring often. Stir in the kale, onion, carrot, celery, and garlic and cook, stirring occasionally, until the vegetables are softened, about 10 minutes.

Add the beans, farro, chicken stock, and tomatoes and bring the liquid to a boil. Stir in the rosemary and sage, adjust the heat down so the liquid is simmering, and cook for 1 hour to 1 hour 10 minutes, until the beans are tender. If the soup is too thick, stir in additional chicken stock as needed. Season to taste with salt and pepper.

Ladle the soup into large bowls, drizzle with extra-virgin olive oil, sprinkle with Parmigiano cheese, and serve immediately.

Borlotti Beans

Borlotti are a large, speckled variety of bean that is one of Tuscany's most well-known legumes. When cooked, their pink and tan markings turn light brown and the beans become meaty and soft. Buy dried beans from sources where there is a high turnover. Old beans require more time to soften.

Zuppa di Lenticchie
Lentil Soup

Lentil soup is another treasured Italian staple.
I prefer the tiny brown lentils from Castelluccio, in Umbria, that are famous for their delicate flavor. If they
are not available, small green French *lentilles du Puy* or any variety of lentils will work.
For this and many other soups, once the ingredients are cooked, I remove about a third of them
and purée them until smooth. The purée that is returned to the pot prevents the liquid
from separating and adds a smooth finish to the soup.

3 cups lentils

¼ cup extra-virgin olive oil

½ cup finely chopped pancetta

1 medium-large yellow onion, diced (1 cup)

1 large carrot, peeled and diced (½ cup)

1 large rib celery, trimmed and diced (½ cup)

3 cloves garlic, thinly sliced, plus 2 whole cloves

6 cups Homemade Chicken Stock (page 255) or canned low-sodium stock

1 cup peeled (see page 105), seeded, and diced tomatoes,
  or substitute diced canned tomatoes, drained

1 sprig fresh rosemary

Sea salt and freshly ground black pepper

4 slices rustic bread, grilled, rubbed with olive oil and garlic (optional)

Rinse and drain the lentils, carefully picking through them to remove any foreign matter. Set aside.
In a large pot, heat the olive oil over medium-high heat until hot. Add the pancetta and cook,
stirring occasionally, to let it render its fat, 2 to 4 minutes. Stir in the onion, carrot, celery, and sliced
garlic and cook, stirring, until the vegetables are softened, about 6 minutes. Add the lentils, chicken

stock, tomatoes, and rosemary and bring the liquid to a boil over high heat.

Adjust the heat down so the liquid is simmering and cook for 25 to 30 minutes. Remove about one-third of the cooked lentils and purée them in a food processor until smooth. Stir the purée into the pot with the remaining soup and season to taste with salt and pepper. If the soup seems too thick, stir in a little water and reheat the soup if needed. Ladle the soup into bowls and serve with grilled bread, if desired.

Cacio e Ovo
Soup of Bitter Greens with Cheese Dumplings

[MAKES 4 TO 6 SERVINGS]

Like many Abruzzese foods, *cacio e ovo*—which means cheese and eggs in Italian—is simply prepared but very satisfying. It is real chicken soup for the soul! The hearty dumplings, a mixture of two cheeses, bread crumbs, and herbs, make it substantial enough to eat as a main course. The uncooked dumplings can be refrigerated overnight.

1 cup lightly packed freshly grated Parmigiano-Reggiano cheese (about 4 ounces)

1 cup lightly packed freshly grated Pecorino Romano cheese (about 4 ounces), plus more for serving

¾ cup fine dried bread crumbs

4 large eggs, lightly beaten

1 tablespoon finely chopped fresh flat-leaf parsley

2 cloves garlic, minced

2 tablespoons extra-virgin olive oil

½ pound bitter greens, such as escarole or chicory, coarse stems removed and discarded, coarsely chopped

2 quarts Homemade Chicken Stock (page 255) or canned low-sodium stock

Sea salt and freshly ground black pepper

In a large bowl, combine the Parmigiano, Pecorino, bread crumbs, eggs, parsley, and half of the garlic and stir until the mixture pulls together into a soft dough. Using moistened hands, roll the mixture into ¾-inch balls and arrange them in a single layer on a baking sheet lined with plastic wrap. Refrigerate until chilled and firm, about 30 minutes.

Meanwhile, in a medium-size saucepan, heat the olive oil over medium-high heat until hot but not smoking. Add the remaining garlic and cook, stirring, until softened, about 30 seconds. Add the greens and cook, stirring, until they are wilted and just beginning to brown, 3 to 4 minutes longer.

Add the stock and bring to a simmer. Drop the dumplings into the simmering stock and cook until they rise to the surface, about 5 minutes. Season the soup with salt and pepper and serve in deep bowls, passing the grated Pecorino at the table.

Crema di Carciofi e Topinambur
Creamy Artichoke and Sunchoke Soup

Artichokes and sunchokes are members of different botanical familiies—artichokes are part of the thistle family, while sunchokes are related to sunflowers—but their complementary nutty flavors add a lovely complexity to this satisfying soup.

1 lemon, halved

4 large artichokes, stemmed

1 pound sunchokes

¼ cup olive oil

¼ pound chopped pancetta

1 small yellow onion, finely chopped (½ cup)

1 small carrot, peeled and finely chopped (¼ cup)

1 small rib celery, trimmed and finely chopped (¼ cup)

3 cloves garlic, minced

2 sprigs fresh marjoram, or substitute fresh oregano or basil

2 sprigs fresh thyme

½ cup dry white wine, such as Pinot Grigio or Sauvignon Blanc

About 4½ cups Homemade Chicken Stock (page 255) or canned low-sodium stock

¼ cup heavy cream

Sea salt and ground white pepper

Sliced crusty bread, for serving

Squeeze the lemon juice into a bowl of cold water and add the lemon halves. Using a sharp knife, cut the artichokes in half crosswise. Working with one artichoke at a time, pull off all the outer green leaves until only the tender yellow leaves remain. Trim off the dark green skin of the heart. Scrape out the hairy

44

choke with a teaspoon, then quarter the heart and drop it into the lemon water.

Peel and coarsely chop the sunchokes. Add them to the artichokes in the lemon water. In a large, heavy nonreactive pot, heat the olive oil until hot. Add the pancetta, onions, carrots, celery, and garlic and cook over medium-high heat, stirring occasionally, until the vegetables are softened, 5 to 6 minutes. Drain the artichokes and sunchokes, add them to the pot along with the marjoram and thyme, and cook for 3 minutes, stirring frequently. Add the white wine, bring the liquid to a boil, and cook until it has almost evaporated.

Add 4 cups of the chicken stock to the pot and simmer until the vegetables are tender, about 30 minutes. Discard the herbs. Add the heavy cream and bring to a simmer. Transfer the soup to an electric blender and purée until smooth. If the soup is too thick, add the remaining ½ cup stock, return it to the pot, and reheat. Season to taste with salt and white pepper and serve with crusty bread.

Sunchokes or Jerusalem Artichokes

Sunchokes are also known as Jerusalem artichokes and top-inambour. They have a lovely nutty taste and can be used both cooked and raw. Store them in the refrigerator. They keep for at least a month.

Carne all'Albese
Minced Tenderloin of Beef with White Truffles

[MAKES 4 SERVINGS]

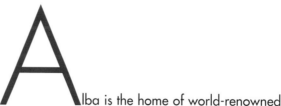

Alba is the home of world-renowned Piemontese white truffles. Besides shaving them over pasta and eggs, locals love to top chopped raw beef—steak tartare—with truffle oil and thinly sliced fresh truffles. It is a dish that I adore.

If you make this dish, it is essential to use the finest quality, freshest beef you can buy because the meat is not cooked. It is frozen for an hour to firm it. Then it is minced by hand with a very sharp knife to ensure that it remains as attractive, toothsome little cubes rather than ground beef. Using a fork to mix it together helps keep the texture nice and loose.

1 pound beef tenderloin or sirloin, trimmed of all fat

2 tablespoons extra-virgin olive oil

2 tablespoons white truffle oil (see Sources, page 266),
   plus a few drops for drizzling

2 tablespoons freshly squeezed lemon juice

¼ cup finely chopped fresh chives or scallions, including green parts

Sea salt and coarsely ground black pepper

4 ounces assorted fresh greens, such as mâche, frisée, and arugula, with
   stems removed, washed, dried, and torn into pieces

1 small piece Parmigiano-Reggiano cheese (about 2 ounces), for shaving

½ ounce white truffles, for shaving (optional)

4 slices Italian bread (about 6 inches in diameter),
   brushed with olive oil and lightly toasted

Wrap the beef in plastic wrap and freeze for an hour to firm up. Remove and, using a very sharp knife, cut it into very small pieces (less than ⅛ inch). Transfer the meat to a metal bowl set it inside another bowl partially filled with some ice and a little water. Add the olive oil, truffle oil, lemon juice, and chives or scallions and gently stir with a fork to combine. Season to taste with salt and pepper and mix again.

Divide the greens among 4 plates and drizzle a little olive oil over them. Divide the meat into 4 equal portions and shape into patties; place 1 patty in the center of each plate of greens. Add shavings of cheese and, if desired, shavings of white truffle over the meat. Add a few drops of truffle oil to each portion, and serve with toasted Italian bread.

paste, polenta e risotto

Basic Pasta *Spaghetti con Fave e Pomodorini*
Spaghetti with Fava Beans and Grape Tomatoes *Spaghetti con Cozze e Zucchine* Spaghetti with Mussels and Zucchini *Tagliolini con Crema di Piave, Speck e Radicchio* Thin Ribbon Pasta with Piave Cream, Speck, and Radicchio *Tagliolini con Gamberi e Astice* Tagliolini with Shrimp and Lobster *Taglietelle con Carciofi* Taglietelle with Artichokes *Pappardelle al Ragù di Coniglio* Pappardelle with Bolognese-Style Braised Rabbit and Parmigiano-Reggiano Cream *Garganelli con Prosciutto, Piselli e Panna* Pasta Quills with San Daniele Prosciutto, Spring Peas, and Cream *Gemelli con Asparagi* Gemelli with Asparagus *Lasagne alla Bolognese* Lasagna with Meat Sauce *Agnolotti con Ricotta e Spinaci* Agnolotti Filled with Ricotta and Spinach *Cappellacci di Zucca con Amaretti e Parmigiano-Reggiano* Pasta Hats Filled with Butternut Squash, Amaretti, and Parmigiano-Reggiano, with Sage Butter Sauce *Tortellini di Coda di Bue* Oxtail Tortellini *Tortelli di Robiola* Robiola Cheese-Filled Tortelli *Gnocchi con Funghi e Fave* Gnocchi with Morels and Fava Beans *Morbidelle con Fonduta al Formaggio* Robiola Cheese with Soft Polenta and Fonduta *Polenta con Rape e Pancetta* Baked Polenta with Sautéed Broccoli Rabe and Pancetta *Risotto alla Pescatora* Fisherman's Risotto

PASTA, POLENTA,
and RISOTTO

Guests at Fiamma rave about our pastas, polentas,

and risottos. While this pleases me, I'm not surprised. We love these dishes because they are supremely comforting and satisfying, particularly when well prepared with quality ingredients and tasty sauces. Even diners who consider this category old hat, or those who eschew carbohydrates for dietary reasons, tell us they have been seduced anew. (During the height of the Atkins or South Beach craze, it's worth noting that very few people did not order pasta.)

I've heard many favorable comments about the silkiness of the wide pappardelle in our heady Braised Rabbit *Ragù* or the creamy-toothsome quality of the rice in our Fisherman-Style Risotto. They emphasize that all of the textures in a dish are important. If the pasta is flabby or flavorless or the rice is gummy, the dish simply can't succeed.

Pasta

Pasta comes in a wide variety of sizes and forms. Most are rolled into flat sheets, then cut in widths from finest angel hair to wide ribbons, or in squares and circles to fold and encase a filling. Others, like penne, are extruded. At Fiamma we make pasta in over twenty shapes, including thin and broad flat pastas and large and small raviolis, as well as gnocchi.

While we make pastas every day, I realize this is not necessarily something home cooks have the time to do or even aspire to. However, I would be remiss if I didn't begin this chapter with my basic pasta recipe. I hope you will attempt to make it at least once or twice to appreciate the difference homemade makes. With a little practice, you will find the techniques easy to master.

My secret to gossamer thin pasta is this: After rolling the dough out on the finest notch of a pasta maker, let it rest for 30 minutes. Then roll it out two more times on that last setting. This is because as you knead pasta, the flour becomes elastic. Stretch the dough and it will rebound. Even when you think the dough is seemingly at its thinnest, it can be rolled thinner yet.

You can buy sheets of fresh pasta or those already cut into spaghetti, etc., from specialty food stores or from the Internet for the recipes in this chapter. (See Sources, page 266.) If you have a pasta machine at home and want to make store-bought sheets thinner and more delicate, crank the sheets through the finest setting of the rollers a couple of times. You will be surprised at the difference this can make.

Although suppliers say fresh pasta can be frozen, I think it is best when refrigerated and used right away. This is especially true with sheets of pasta because they tend to become brittle after freezing. Extruded pastas, like rigatoni and penne, are impossible to make at home unless you have an electric pasta machine with the right attachment. Even in Italy they are typically bought either fresh or dried.

For dried pasta, the ones from Barilla and DeCecco, sold in many supermarkets across America, have impressed me the most. I haven't found those in fancy packaging tied with straw ribbons to be of any better quality. You are simply paying more for them. Also, colored pasta isn't used much in Italy. That fad is dying out here, too. It is decorative, but nothing more.

When cooking dried pasta, most people follow the directions on the box that say it should boil for 11 to 12 minutes to become al dente. That is fine except they don't realize that if pasta is drained at that point and put into the sauce, it might easily sit in it for up to 15 minutes before arriving at the table. By then, the pasta will be overcooked and won't combine correctly with the sauce.

To ensure that the pasta and sauce bond, I like to remove the pasta 2 to 3 minutes before it is even al dente and toss it into the pot with the sauce. The pasta finishes cooking by absorbing the liquid and ends up being perfectly cooked. In Italy, they say the pasta is *tirata*, or tightened. This works best with dried pastas where you have longer cooking times and don't risk overcooking.

Another technique that works quite well is to pour the cooked sauce into a large, wide metal bowl. Once the pasta is cooked and drained, it is added to the sauce and tossed. The metal bowl keeps the sauce warm and makes it quite easy to serve the dish.

There is an art to pairing the right type, thickness, and shape of pasta with a sauce. A light sauce combines best with smaller or finer pasta. At home, one of my favorite dishes is fresh spaghetti tossed with the finest-quality melted butter and grated Parmigiano-Reggiano I can buy. The thin pasta does not overshadow the delicate sauce. Similarly, long, narrow *tagliolini* noodles, usually less than 1/8 inch wide, used with shrimp, lobster, and sliced vegetables in a delicate white wine and herb broth (page 65) blend harmoniously. (*Tagliolini* is also called *tagliarini*.)

Prosciutto-scented, truffled cream sauce tossed with peas and Parmigiano-Reggiano cheese is a more substantial mixture, so tubular quills, or *garganelli*, are a good choice of pasta. The quills' ridges capture every last drop of the rich sauce and the short shape complements the shape of the peas and small pieces of ham. And wide *pappardelle* ribbons simply lap up the luxurious rabbit *ragù* on page 70.

Before serving a dish, taste all the components with the pasta. It is sometimes surprising how the flavors impact one another. The sauce should lightly coat each strand, rather than burying or overwhelming it.

In this chapter, I use classic and more contemporary Italian ingredients in the recipes, as well as American ingredients in an Italian style. Meaty oxtails and high-quality canned tomatoes for tortellini have long been available to American shoppers. Rapini and fava beans—familiar in Italy—are becoming more readily available.

I also introduce ingredients like *speck*, the salt- and smoke-cured ham from Trentino's Alto Adige, and *mostarda*, the piquant preserved fruit-mustard condiment from Cremona, that are just arriving on the horizon in this country. These provisions are now available from some of the sources mentioned at the end of the book, starting on page 266.

There are basic dishes like Spaghetti with Grape Tomatoes and Fava Beans that taste fresh and modern. Others are dishes with old roots, like Ravioli filled with Butternut Squash, Amaretti, and Parmigiano with Brown Butter and Sage that have been made in Mantua for centuries. While most are very simple to prepare, a few are time consuming. I assure you, the results will be well worth your efforts.

Finally, a word about portion sizes. In Italy pasta is traditionally served as a separate course before the main dish. Americans order pasta both as the middle course after the antipasto and as an entrée. The recipes in this chapter are generous; most may be served as a main course. How many each will serve depends on your appetite and what else is included in the meal.

Polenta

Quick cooking or instant polentas are easy to find in your supermarket and produce reasonable results. To me, however, they cannot compare with cornmeal that is slowly simmered with nothing more than salt and water. At most, I add a little butter at the end.

I realize the traditional method takes time, from 45 minutes to an hour. But shortcuts—using quick-cooking polenta and/or adding a lot of Parmigiano or even mascarpone cheese and butter to make it smooth—essentially blunt the wonderful, earthy taste of the corn; you cannot feel the satisfying granular-but-smooth texture from each little grain. This is a good example of how all the tastes and textures play a role in my cooking.

When making polenta, start by rapidly whisking the cornmeal into boiling liquid to prevent lumps from forming. After about 15 minutes, when the polenta starts to thicken, change to a large wooden spoon or spatula with a flat bottom to scrape the bottom of the pan as you stir. Keep cooking until the water is absorbed, the polenta is bubbling, and it glistens.

Polenta recipes will call for more or less liquid, depending on how stiff you want it to be. Three cups of liquid added to a cup of cornmeal will be creamy; if you use two cups, the results will be quite firm. Cooking time averages 45 minutes to an hour. Once you create the crust (*la crosta*) on the bottom of a heavy pan, the polenta will bubble but will not burn. Just give it an occasional stir.

Risotto

By now, Americans are champions at making risotto-like dishes with everything from Arborio to long-grain American rice and even barley. But if you don't know why the broth is heated and then slowly added to the simmering rice ladle by ladle, let me remind you. It slowly melts and coaxes the starch from each grain, producing the creamy-toothsome texture essential to the dish's success.

When risotto includes seafood, Italians do not typically serve cheese with it. Nor do I. Once you prepare the Fisherman's Risotto on page 97, I think you will agree that it has plenty of tastes without any Parmigiano. A final note: In the seafood risotto, as well as in many pasta and risotto dishes, I often add a final drizzle of olive oil to the dish before serving as an appealing, shiny glaze.

Basic Pasta

[MAKES ABOUT 1 POUND OF DOUGH]

Homemade pasta really is better than anything you can buy. Make it a couple of times and I think you will agree. For the final product to be very tender, it is essential that the dough rest for thirty minutes to an hour before being rolled for the last time. Freshly made pasta dries out quickly when left out. This does affect the cooking time but not the taste, tenderness, or quality. Within an hour of being made, it will take minimal cooking time—as little as thirty seconds. This increases to five to seven minutes after a few hours. Always taste pasta during cooking to determine when it reaches the al dente stage.

$2\frac{1}{4}$ cups all-purpose flour, plus more as needed

3 large eggs, at room temperature

1 tablespoon extra-virgin olive oil

Pinch of sea salt

Mound 2 cups of the flour in the center of a large wooden board and make a well in the center. Beat the eggs, oil, and salt together in a small bowl, and pour them into the well. Using a fork, begin incorporating the flour into the eggs, a little at a time, working from the outside edges. The dough will come together and be lumpy, but don't worry.

When the dough becomes too stiff to mix with a fork, dust your hands with flour and begin kneading it. Sprinkle more flour onto the dough and knead until it is no longer wet and sticky. Once it becomes smooth and somewhat stiff, lightly flour the board and continue kneading for 3 to 5 minutes more, until the dough becomes elastic. Knead it for 4 more minutes, always dusting the board and your hands with flour, if necessary. Divide the dough in half, flatten it into small rectangles of a size to fit through a hand-crank pasta machine, wrap in plastic wrap, and set aside for 1 hour at room temperature to rest.

On a hand-crank pasta machine, adjust the rollers to the widest setting. Working with one rectangle of dough at a time, feed the dough through the rollers. Remove and lightly dust with flour. Fold the strip into thirds, flatten it with your fingertips, and pass it through the machine at least twice more, or until the dough is very smooth and the edges are even, lightly dusting with flour each time.

Once the pasta is silky and smooth, do not flour it.

Adjusting the rollers to ever-narrower settings, continue rolling the dough until it is as thin as needed, usually the last or next to last setting. As the strips become increasingly longer, take care not to pull or stretch them. The easiest way to hold the strip is to drape it between your left thumb and forefinger while cranking with the right hand.

Cut the strips into 18-inch lengths. After rolling the pasta on the narrowest setting, cover the strips with a clean cloth and let them rest for 30 minutes to an hour, then roll twice more through the narrowest setting. Cut the sheets according to the recipe, into squares for *agnolotti, cappellacci,* etc., or use them whole for lasagna. For fettuccini or spaghetti, change the rollers to cut the sheets into the size pasta you desire.

If not cooking the pasta immediately, spread it on clean, dry towels and lightly dust with flour, tossing to separate the strands, or hang it over a pasta drying rack or kitchen chair. Repeat with the remaining dough.

Spaghetti con Fave e Pomodorini
Spaghetti with Fava Beans and Grape Tomatoes

[MAKES 4 SERVINGS]

Spaghetti with fava beans, fresh tomatoes, and basil is a combination that sings summertime on a plate. I love grape tomatoes for their oval shape and the intense sweet taste they add to dishes. Flat fava beans are another favorite of mine. Once removed from their pod, the beans look like large limas. You need to blanch them to remove the tough outer skin before cooking. When they come to market in late spring, fava beans are small and green. Look for them in Mediterranean and Middle Eastern markets. In southern Italy, they are so tiny and tender, the inner shells don't need to be removed. See the sidebar for how to prepare them.

½ cup extra-virgin olive oil, plus extra for drizzling

4 cloves garlic, thinly sliced

2 cups grape tomatoes, quartered

¾ cup loosely packed, julienned basil leaves

2½ to 3 pounds fava beans, shelled and blanched
(to net 1 pound beans; see sidebar)

Sea salt and freshly ground black pepper

1 pound Basic Pasta (page 55), cut as spaghetti, or store-bought
fresh or dried pasta

¼ cup freshly grated Parmigiano-Reggiano cheese (optional)

In a large skillet, heat the ½ cup of olive oil over medium heat until warm. Add the garlic and cook, stirring, over low heat for 1 to 2 minutes just until it is soft but not colored, shaking the pan once or twice; stir in the tomatoes and cook for 1 minute, crushing them with a wooden spoon. Sprinkle in the basil, then add the fava beans, and cook just to warm the beans through. Season to taste with salt and pepper and pour into a large metal bowl.

Bring a large pot of salted water to a boil. Stir in the pasta and cook until al dente, about 2 minutes for fresh pasta. For dried pasta, follow the manufacturer's directions. Drain the pasta, leaving a small amount of water on the pasta, and toss it with the tomatoes and fava beans in the bowl, turning to blend well. Divide the pasta among 4 plates and sprinkle with the cheese. Drizzle with the remaining olive oil and serve immediately.

Buying and Shelling Fava Beans

When buying fresh fava beans, 2½ to 3 pounds will yield about a pound of shelled beans. Look for beans with pods that appear full, not shriveled, and that don't reveal the beans underneath. There should be no more than 7 to 8 beans inside.

Start by shelling the favas and discarding the pods. Cook them in boiling salted water until tender, 2 to 3 minutes. Drain and shock in ice water to cool. Then drain and peel off the outer skin by gently squeezing the end of each bean between your thumb and pointer finger to remove it. They will keep for several days in the refrigerator in a covered bowl.

Spaghetti con Cozze e Zucchine
Spaghetti with Mussels and Zucchini

Deep-green zucchini slices, shiny black mussels in their shells, and tomatoes make for an appealingly colorful spaghetti dish that is the epitome of simplicity to prepare. The flavors are emboldened with a pinch or more of red pepper flakes added to the pot. Because there is nothing to camouflage inferior tastes, every ingredient should be the finest you can find.

¼ cup extra-virgin olive oil

3 cloves garlic, thinly sliced

Pinch of red pepper flakes

2 pounds Prince Edward Island mussels, scrubbed and debearded

2 cups dry white wine, such as Pinot Grigio

1 large zucchini, cut in half lengthwise and thinly sliced (about 2 cups)

1 cup grape tomatoes, quartered, or 2 Roma tomatoes, peeled (see page 105), seeded, and diced

Sea salt and freshly ground black pepper

1 pound Basic Pasta (page 55), cut as spaghetti, or store-bought fresh or dried pasta

2 tablespoons julienned flat-leaf parsley, plus additional for garnish

In a saucepan with a tight-fitting lid, heat the olive oil over medium-high heat. Stir in the garlic and pepper flakes and cook for 1 minute. Add the mussels and white wine, cover, and cook until the mussels open, 2 to 3 minutes. Discard any that do not open.

Add the zucchini and tomatoes, cover, and cook, stirring occasionally, for 3 minutes more. Season to taste with salt and pepper; keep warm over low heat.

Bring a large pot of salted water to a boil. Stir in the pasta and cook until al dente, 2 to 3 minutes for fresh pasta, then drain. For dried pasta, follow the manufacturer's directions. Turn the sauce into a large metal bowl, add the spaghetti and sliced parsley, and toss to combine. Divide the pasta among 4 large, flat bowls, garnish with a little parsley, and serve.

Grape Tomatoes

Grape tomatoes have the oval shape of the fruit they are named for and are particularly sweet. Although more expensive than cherry tomatoes, they are a treat. If you grow tomatoes in your garden, look for varieties like Santa Claus, Christmas, and Juliette at plant stores or online. If well staked and supported, the prolific plants can grow to over seven feet tall. They bear fruit from June through the beginning of October, depending on the climate.

Tagliolini con Crema di Piave, Speck e Radicchio
Thin Ribbon Pasta with Piave Cream, Speck, and Radicchio

[MAKES 4 SERVINGS]

I think of this pasta sauce as *fonduta* for 2006 (see page 92). It is light, contemporary Italian cooking at its best with lots of rich flavors but made with less butter and cream. The velvety smooth, creamy base is created by rapidly blending boiling hot stock and olive oil into hay-colored *piave* cheese. The temperature is essential to quickly melt the cheese. The pasta is flavored with *speck*—the assertive-tasting, smoky ham of the Alto Adige or Süd Tirol region—and bitter radicchio.

1½ cups grated *piave* cheese or Parmigiano-Reggiano cheese, plus extra for grating at the end

1½ cups boiling Homemade Chicken Stock (page 255) or canned low-sodium stock

2 tablespoons extra-virgin olive oil, plus extra for drizzling

2 teaspoons white truffle oil (optional, see Sources, page 266)

4 tablespoons (½ stick) unsalted butter

¼ cup finely diced yellow onion

2 cloves garlic, sliced

2 cups julienned radicchio leaves

6 ounces *speck*, julienned, or substitute smoked ham

1 teaspoon fresh thyme leaves

Sea salt and freshly ground black pepper

1 pound Basic Pasta (page 55), cut as *tagliolini* (about ⅛ inch wide), or store-bought fresh or dried pasta

Put all but 2 tablespoons of the 1½ cups of grated cheese in a large, deep, heat-resistant bowl. Pour ½ cup of boiling chicken stock over the cheese and, using an immersion blender, blend on high speed until the cheese begins to melt. Or transfer the mixture to the jar of an electric blender and blend on high speed.

With the blender running, add the 2 tablespoons olive oil and the truffle oil, if using, and continue blending until the sauce is smooth and emulsified. When blended, pour the sauce into a small pan, cover, and keep warm over very low heat.

In a large skillet, melt the butter over medium-high heat. Add the onion and garlic and cook, stirring, until the onion is translucent, 1 to 2 minutes. Stir in the radicchio, speck, the remaining 1 cup of boiling chicken stock, and thyme. Return to a boil, then adjust the heat down to medium-low and simmer until heated through, 2 to 3 minutes. Season to taste with salt and pepper. Keep warm.

Bring a large pot of salted water to a boil. Stir in the pasta and cook until al dente, about 2 minutes for fresh pasta, then drain. For dried pasta, follow the manufacturer's directions.

While the pasta is boiling, remove the sauce from the heat. Stir in the reserved 2 tablespoons of grated *piave* cheese. Add the pasta to the sauce and turn to coat evenly. Divide the pasta among 4 warmed large plates. Sprinkle with a little additional cheese and freshly ground black pepper, drizzle a little olive oil over the pasta, and serve at once.

Piave Cheese

Piave is a traditional cow's milk cheese from Belluno, an Alpine region of Italy with rich green pastures. The dense, pale flax-colored cheese is made from both the rich morning milking and partially skimmed evening milking. The mild, slightly sweet cheese is popular both as a table cheese, particularly when it is fresh, and for grating once it has matured and hardened. I like to use it in pasta dishes and salads.

Tagliolini con Gamberi e Astice
Tagliolini with Shrimp and Lobster

[MAKES 4 SERVINGS]

Even before you take a bite, this dish will tempt your senses. Chunks of lobster in bright red shells are tossed with shrimp, tomatoes, zucchini, and ribbons of *tagliolini*. It suggests the vivid colors of the Italian flag. The fragrant sauce is a complex marriage of brandy, white wine, and the essence of shellfish accented by a hint of tarragon. Although I appreciate the taste of tarragon in cooked foods, when used raw I find the herb's licorice flavor too assertive. Instead, I use flat-leaf parsley for the garnish here. If you cannot buy fresh lobster claws, you can use all tails or use slowly defrosted frozen lobster tails.

½ cup extra-virgin olive oil

1½ pounds uncooked Maine lobster tails or claws, in the shell, preferably fresh, with the tails split down the center and cut into 1-inch pieces

20 jumbo shrimp, peeled and deveined

3 cloves garlic, thinly sliced

1 medium zucchini, thinly sliced (2 cups)

¼ cup brandy

2 cups grape or cherry tomatoes, quartered

2 tablespoons chopped fresh tarragon

Pinch of red pepper flakes

½ cup dry white wine, such as Pinot Grigio or Trebbiano

Sea salt and freshly ground black pepper

1 pound Basic Pasta (page 55), cut as *tagliolini* (about ⅛ inch wide), or store-bought fresh or dried pasta

Julienned flat-leaf parsley, for garnish

Heat the olive oil in a large deep skillet over medium-high heat. Add the lobster pieces and sauté until they turn red, about 1 minute, shaking the pan often. Add the shrimp, season to taste with salt and pepper, and sauté until they turn pink.

Stir in the garlic and zucchini and continue cooking, stirring occasionally, until the zucchini is translucent, 2 to 3 minutes. Pour in the brandy and scrape up any browned bits with a wooden spoon. Turn the heat to high and carefully ignite the liquid. When the flames subside, stir in the tomatoes, tarragon, pepper flakes, and white wine. Bring the liquid to a boil and cook until reduced by half, about 2 minutes. Season to taste with salt and pepper. Transfer the sauce to a large metal bowl.

Bring a large pot of salted water to a boil. Stir in the pasta and cook until al dente, 2 to 3 minutes for fresh pasta. Drain the pasta. For dried pasta, follow the manufacturer's directions.
Add the pasta to the bowl with the lobster and shrimp sauce, and gently toss. Taste to adjust the seasonings, divide among 4 plates, and serve immediately garnished with a little parsley.

Taglietelle con Carciofi
Taglietelli with Artichokes

[MAKES 4 SERVINGS]

In this pleasantly light dish, *taglietelli*—thin ribbons of pasta about ¼ inch wide—are combined with artichoke hearts simmered in white wine and rich chicken stock. This refined pasta is well suited to serve before a substantial main course. Fettuccine may be substituted for *taglietelli*.

¼ pound pancetta, cut into ¼-inch cubes

2 tablespoons extra-virgin olive oil

1 small yellow onion, chopped (½ cup)

4 cloves garlic, peeled and crushed

6 medium artichokes hearts, thinly sliced (see sidebar)

Sea salt and freshly ground black pepper

Generous pinch of red pepper flakes

½ cup dry white wine, such as Pinot Grigio or Trebbiano

¾ cups Rich Chicken Stock (page 256), plus extra if needed

¼ cup loosely packed chopped basil leaves, plus small leaves for garnish

1 pound Basic Pasta (page 55), cut as *taglietelli,* or
store-bought fresh or dried pasta

½ cup freshly grated Parmigiano-Reggiano cheese, plus
cheese for sprinkling

In a large deep skillet, sauté the pancetta in the olive oil over medium-high heat until very lightly browned, 5 to 6 minutes, shaking the pan or stirring frequently. Add the onion and garlic and cook, stirring, until the onion is translucent, about 3 minutes. Add the artichokes and a pinch of salt and cook, stirring, until lightly browned, 3 to 5 minutes.

Add the pepper flakes, cook for 1 minute, then stir in the white wine and bring the liquid to a boil over high heat. Cook until the wine has almost completely evaporated, then add the stock and basil and cook over medium heat until the artichokes are very tender, 15 to 20 minutes, stirring or shaking the pan occasionally. Pour into a large metal bowl and season generously with salt and pepper.

Bring a large pot of salted water to a boil. Stir in the pasta and cook until al dente, 2 to 3 minutes for fresh pasta. Drain well. For dried pasta, follow the manufacturer's directions. Add the pasta to the bowl with the artichoke-broth mixture along with the cheese and toss. If the pasta seems dry, add a small amount of hot stock. Divide the pasta among 4 large plates, sprinkle with cheese, garnish with a couple of basil leaves, and serve.

Preparing Artichoke Hearts

Cut off the stem of each artichoke flush with the bottom. Cut about 1 inch off the top. Snap off the leaves, by turning them backward, and discard. With a sharp paring knife, slice off the woody parts that remain surrounding the heart. Using a vegetable peeler or sharp paring knife, scrape out the hairy choke. Once the choke is removed, the heart will discolor quickly, so rub it with lemon juice as it is trimmed or drop the hearts into a bowl of water with the juice of one half lemon added to it.

Pappardelle al Ragù di Coniglio
Pappardelle with Bolognese-Style Braised Rabbit and Parmigiano-Reggiano Cream

[MAKES 6 SERVINGS AS A MIDDLE COURSE;
MAKES 4 SERVINGS AS AN ENTRÉE]

appardelle are wide ribbons of pasta. They are the ideal partner for luscious morsels of tender, braised rabbit. Hidden under the pasta and thinner-than-normal sauce is a smooth, nutty Parmigiano cream that adds a contemporary, rich element to this rustic dish and thickens the sauce beautifully.

One 2½- to 3-pound rabbit, rinsed, cut into serving pieces,
and patted dry with paper towels

Sea salt and freshly ground black pepper

9 tablespoons extra-virgin olive oil

1 tablespoon unsalted butter

1 medium-large yellow onion, chopped (1 cup)

1 large carrot, peeled and chopped (½ cup)

1 large rib celery, trimmed and chopped (½ cup)

3 plum or Roma tomatoes, cored and chopped (about 2 cups)

2 to 3 cloves garlic, crushed

2 sprigs fresh rosemary

2 sprigs fresh sage, with 10 to 15 leaves

1 cup white wine, such as Pinot Grigio or Trebbiano

4½ cups Rich Chicken Stock (page 256)

1½ cups freshly grated Parmigiano-Reggiano cheese

1 pound Basic Pasta, (page 55), cut into *pappardelle* (about 1 inch wide),
or store-bought fresh or dried *pappardelle*

2 tablespoons chopped flat-leaf parsley

Preheat the oven to 375°F.

Season the rabbit generously with salt and pepper. In a large Dutch oven or deep pot, heat 4 tablespoons of the olive oil over medium-high heat until almost smoking. Working in two batches, add the rabbit, flesh side down, and cook until richly browned on one side, 4 to 5 minutes. Turn and cook the second side for the same amount of time until browned. Transfer the rabbit to a large bowl as the pieces are done. If necessary, add 2 more tablespoons of oil for the second batch.

Reduce the heat to medium and add the butter to the pot. Add the onion, carrot, and celery and cook, stirring occasionally and scraping up any browned bits from the bottom, until the vegetables are tender and begin to caramelize, 6 to 8 minutes. Return the rabbit along with the tomatoes, garlic, rosemary, and sage to the pot and cook, stirring occasionally, for 1 to 2 minutes.

Pour in the white wine, turn the heat to medium-high, and bring the liquid to a boil. Cook until the liquid is reduced by half, 8 to 10 minutes. Pour in 4 cups of chicken stock, bring to a simmer, cover the pan tightly, and transfer to the oven for 45 minutes to 1 hour, until the rabbit is tender when pierced with a fork. Transfer the meat to a cutting board to cool slightly, tenting it lightly with aluminum foil.

Strain the liquid into a medium bowl, wipe out the Dutch oven, then return the braising liquid to the pot. Bring to a boil over medium-high heat and boil until reduced by half, 25 to 30 minutes. Meanwhile, cut the meat from the bones, tear it into large pieces, and then add it to the reduced sauce. Season to taste with salt and pepper. Keep warm over the lowest heat.

Bring the remaining ½ cup of chicken stock to a rolling boil. Put 1 cup of the grated cheese into a deep heat-proof bowl. Pour the boiling stock over the cheese, beating it with a hand-held electric blender or whisking until smooth. Slowly drizzle in the remaining 3 tablespoons of olive oil, whisking constantly, and set aside. The Parmigiano-Reggiano cream will thicken considerably as it sits.

Bring a large pot of salted water to a boil. Add the *pappardelle* and cook until al dente, 2 to 3 minutes for fresh pasta. For dried pasta, follow the manufacturer's directions. Drain well and stir into the sauce.

To serve, divide the Parmigiano-Reggiano cream among 4 large flat soup bowls. Spoon the *pappardelle* and rabbit onto the cream, sprinkle with parsley and the remaining ½ cup of cheese, and serve immediately.

Garganelli con Prosciutto, Piselli e Panna
Pasta Quills with San Daniele Prosciutto, Spring Peas, and Cream

[MAKES 4 SERVINGS]

In this luxurious dish, tubular quills, or *garganelli,* are bathed in prosciutto-scented, truffled cream sauce and tossed with fresh peas and Parmigiano-Reggiano cheese. The ridges of these elongated tubes capture every last drop of flavor and the short shape complements the creamy sauce.

Garganelli originated in the Romagna region of Italy. The name comes from the Latin *"gargala,"* meaning trachea or windpipe. While similar to penne, the ridges in *garganelli* are horizontal rather than vertical. Imported San Daniele prosciutto is lower in salt than most products made in America. I like to use it in cooking because the dishes don't taste overly salty.

1 pound fresh *garganelli* pasta (see headnote) or
  store-bought fresh or dried *garganelli* or penne rigate

1½ cups heavy cream

8 tablespoons Truffle Butter (page 264), or store-bought

½ pound thinly sliced San Daniele prosciutto, julienned

¾ cup peeled and blanched fresh peas or petite frozen peas, defrosted

Sea salt

1 tablespoon white truffle oil (optional; see Sources, page 266)

¼ cup freshly grated Parmigiano-Reggiano cheese

Bring a large pot of salted water to a boil. Stir in the pasta, cook until almost al dente, 3 to 4 minutes, then drain. Set aside. (If using dried pasta, cook for 10 to 11 minutes.)

In a heavy saucepan, bring the cream to a simmer over medium heat. Add the truffle butter, prosciutto, peas, and the reserved pasta; turn the heat to high and cook until the sauce coats the pasta, shaking the pan vigorously to prevent sticking. Season to taste with salt, add the truffle oil, if using, and the grated cheese, and toss. Serve immediately.

Gemelli con Asparagi
Gemelli with Asparagus

[MAKES 6 SERVINGS]

Gemelli are twin strands of tubular pasta twisted together into a spiral shape. When tossed with prosciutto, grilled asparagus, radishes, and Pecorino *pepato* the combination makes a vivid room-temperature salad.

Pecorino *pepato* is sheep's milk cheese with whole black peppercorns embedded. The sharp-tasting, aged cheese comes from the town of Ragusa in southern Italy. All Italian sheep's milk cheeses are called Pecorino. Those from around Rome are called Pecorino Romano. Others varieties of Pecorino include Toscano (Tuscan) and Siciliano (Sicilian).

1 pound thin asparagus, woody ends removed

¾ cup extra-virgin olive oil, plus extra for brushing

1 pound *gemelli* pasta

6 ounces prosciutto, julienned

1 small bunch radishes, trimmed, thinly sliced, and soaked in ice water to crisp

6 ounces Pecorino *pepato,* shaved

½ cup lightly packed torn basil

¼ cup balsamic vinegar

2 tablespoons Dijon mustard

2 large eggs, hard-cooked and finely chopped

Sea salt and freshly ground black pepper

Brush the asparagus lightly with oil. Light a gas or charcoal grill or heat a large grill pan over medium-high heat. Add the asparagus in batches and grill until just tender, turning occasionally to cook all sides, 5 to 7 minutes. Set aside to cool. Cut into thin diagonal slices and put them in a large bowl.

Meanwhile, bring a large pot of salted water to a boil. Stir in the *gemelli* and cook according to the manufacturer's directions until al dente, 11 to 12 minutes. Drain, rinse under cold water, and drain again. Add to the bowl with the asparagus along with the radishes, Pecorino, and basil leaves.

Combine the ¾ cup of olive oil, the vinegar, mustard, and eggs in the jar of an electric blender and blend until smooth, adding more vinegar, if needed, to adjust the acidity. Pour on the salad and toss. Season to taste with salt and pepper, toss again, and serve.

Lasagne alla Bolognese
Lasagna with Meat Sauce

[MAKES 8 SERVINGS, 7 CUPS SAUCE]

You can dress pasta up or make it very modern in style, but serve traditional lasagna—with layers of Bolognese meat and tomato sauce and creamy béchamel sauce—and few people won't succumb to its charms. In this recipe, I add the canned tomatoes one at a time, crushing them with my hands as I go, to enhance the texture of the sauce. Both sauces for the lasagna may be made a day before and refrigerated in covered containers.

Meat and Tomato Sauce

¼ cup extra-virgin olive oil

1 small yellow onion, diced (½ cup)

1 small carrot, peeled and diced (¼ cup)

1 small rib celery, trimmed and diced (¼ cup)

¼ cup tomato paste

Two 28-ounce cans whole peeled tomatoes, undrained

Sea salt and freshly ground black pepper

½ pound ground beef

½ pound ground pork

½ pound ground veal

1 sprig fresh rosemary

1 sprig fresh sage

2 bay leaves

Parmigiano-Reggiano rind, 2 to 4 inches (optional)

Béchamel Sauce

7 tablespoons unsalted butter, plus butter to grease the pan

½ cup plus 1 tablespoon all-purpose flour

Agnolotti con Ricotta e Spinaci
Agnolotti Filled with Ricotta and Spinach

[MAKES 4 SERVINGS]

In the Piemonte region, little raviolis are known as *agnolotti*. These plump pillows of pasta, filled with ricotta, spinach, and Parmigiano-Reggiano, have attractive zigzagged edges. Once stuffed, the squares are folded a second time and the short ends are crimped, creating a small pocket to capture the hearty wild mushroom sauce.

Agnolotti

2 pounds fresh spinach, washed, dried, and stems removed

¾ pound (1½ cups) fresh whole milk ricotta cheese

½ cup freshly grated Parmigiano-Reggiano cheese

2 large eggs, lightly beaten

Pinch of freshly grated nutmeg

Sea salt and freshly ground black pepper

1 pound Basic Pasta (page 55), rolled to the thinnest setting, or store-bought pasta sheets (see Sources, page 266)

Sauce

2 tablespoons extra-virgin olive oil

3 cloves garlic, crushed

1 pound mixed wild mushrooms, wiped, trimmed, and thinly sliced

1 teaspoon sea salt, or to taste

Freshly ground black pepper

1 cup dry white wine, such as Pinot Grigio or Trebbiano

4 cups Veal Stock (page 258) or Homemade Chicken Stock (page 255) or canned low-sodium stock

continued

79

One sprig fresh rosemary

1 tablespoon unsalted butter

Freshly grated Parmigiano-Reggiano cheese

1 tablespoon julienned flat-leaf parsley

To make the Agnolotti:

Blanch the spinach in a large pot of salted boiling water until bright green and tender, about 1 minute. Drain and shock under cold water. Using your hands, squeeze as much moisture as possible from the spinach, then coarsely chop. In a large mixing bowl, combine the spinach, ricotta cheese, Parmigiano-Reggiano cheese, eggs, and nutmeg. Season to taste with salt and pepper and set aside to cool.

On a lightly floured work surface, using a sharp knife or pizza cutter and ruler, trim the pasta into a 6- x 18-inch rectangle. Cut the pasta into twenty-seven 2-inch squares: First cut it horizontally into three 2-inch strips, then cut it vertically into nine 2-inch widths.

Spoon 1½ teaspoons of the filling in a horizontal line about 1¼ inches long in the center of each square, leaving a border on both sides. Using a spray mister filled with water, lightly mist the pasta with water. Bring the bottom edge of each square up to match the top edge and press around the three cut edges to seal. Bring the lower (folded) edge up to the top edge and press both sides to seal, forming a small horizontal pocket at the top. Using a zigzag pasta wheel, trim about ¼ inch from both sides of each *agnolotti*, taking care not to cut into the filling. Set the *agnolotti* on a baking pan lined with parchment and dusted with a little flour and/or cornmeal. Leave in a cool, dry spot. Continue with the remaining *agnolotti*. (They may be frozen at this point.)

To prepare the Sauce:

In a large heavy skillet, heat the olive oil over medium-high heat. Add the garlic and cook, stirring, until softened and just beginning to color, about 1 minute. Stir in the mushrooms, season with salt and pepper, and cook, stirring frequently, for 1 to 2 minutes. Turn the heat to high, pour in the wine, and deglaze the pan, scraping up any brown bits with a wooden spoon; simmer until the liquid is reduced by half, 6 to 8 minutes.

Add the stock and rosemary sprig. Bring the liquid to a boil, then reduce the heat and simmer for 45 minutes to 1 hour, until the sauce lightly coats the back of a wooden spoon. Taste to adjust the seasonings and keep warm.

Meanwhile, bring a large pot of salted water to a boil. Add the pasta, stir gently, and cook until the *agnolotti* rise to the surface, then cook for 1 minute longer. Remove with a slotted spoon to a large bowl. Drain any water that accumulates in the bowl. Stir in the butter, then add the sauce and a generous amount of Parmigiano-Reggiano, toss to blend, and serve immediately on large plates.

Cappellacci di Zucca con Amaretti e Parmigiano-Reggiano
Pasta Hats Filled with Butternut Squash, Amaretti, and Parmigiano-Reggiano, with Sage Butter Sauce

[MAKES 4 SERVINGS]

In Mantua, in Lombardy, the sweet and savory combination of butternut squash, crushed amaretti, and Parmigiano-Reggiano cheese has been used to fill pasta since medieval times. The sweetness of the squash and amaretti contrast elegantly with the saltiness of the cheese and the subtle bitterness of fresh sage and nutty brown butter. These *cappellacci* are usually served during autumn when pumpkins and squashes come to market. The optional *mostarda* gives a wonderful boost of flavor; the condiment is sold at some specialty food stores, and my recipe for it is on page 263.

1 medium-size butternut squash (about 2 pounds), split lengthwise, seeds and membranes removed

2 teaspoons olive oil

2 large eggs

½ cup freshly grated Parmigiano-Reggiano cheese, plus cheese for sprinkling

¼ teaspoon freshly grated nutmeg

¼ teaspoon cayenne pepper

¾ cup finely crushed amaretti cookies

Sea salt and freshly ground black pepper

1 pound Basic Pasta (page 55), rolled on thinnest setting, or store-bought pasta sheets

continued

4 tablespoons (½ stick) unsalted butter

10 fresh sage leaves

1 to 2 tablespoons *mostarda* (optional; see Sources, page 266,
or recipe, page 263)

Preheat the oven to 375°F.

Brush the squash with olive oil and roast it, flesh side down, on a sheet pan until tender and lightly browned on top, about 45 minutes. Remove from the oven and, when cool enough to handle, scoop out the flesh and discard the skin.

In a large bowl, mash the squash with a potato masher or fork until smooth. Add the eggs, cheese, nutmeg, cayenne, and ½ cup of the crushed amaretti cookies and mix well. Season to taste with salt and pepper, cover, and refrigerate until ready to use.

Working with 2 sheets of pasta on a lightly floured work surface, use a sharp knife or pizza cutter and ruler to cut the first sheet of pasta in half horizontally, then cut it vertically into 3-inch strips to make 12 squares. Repeat with the second sheet. Spoon a teaspoonful of filling in the center of each square. Using a spray mister filled with water, lightly mist the pasta with water, then fold each square in half diagonally to form a triangle, pressing outward from the filling to seal the pasta tightly. Holding each triangle with the sealed top edges up, bring the two bottom side points forward and overlap them by about ½ inch; press to seal. Set the little hats standing up on a sheet pan lined with parchment and dusted with a little flour and/or cornmeal. Leave in a cool, dry spot. Continue folding all the *cappellacci.*

Bring a large pot of salted water to a boil. Add the *cappellacci,* cook until they rise to the surface, then cook for 1 minute longer. Remove with a slotted spoon to a large bowl and set aside.

Melt the butter in a large skillet over medium-high heat and cook until it turns a rich nut brown, 2½ to 3 minutes. Add the sage leaves and turn once or twice. Drain any water that has accumulated at the bottom of the bowl of *cappellacci.* Add the *cappellacci* to the pan and toss to coat evenly with the butter. Transfer to a serving platter, sprinkle with cheese and the remaining ¼ cup of amaretti cookies, and serve immediately. Pass a small bowl of *mostarda,* if using.

Substitutions for Butternut Squash

When butternut squash roasts in the oven, the moisture is reduced and the squash's natural sugar caramelizes to intensify the sweet flavor. If you don't have time to roast it, or you can't find the squash, substitute canned unsweetened pumpkin or even defrosted frozen butternut squash. To remove some of the moisture—which can cause the pasta to become gummy—drain the squash in a strainer lined with a couple of layers of cheesecloth for at least an hour.

Tortellini di Coda di Bue
Oxtail Tortellini

[MAKES 6 TO 8 SERVINGS
FOR A MAIN COURSE]

Braised oxtails or short ribs make a sumptuous filling for tortellini. While the pasta and sauce take time to prepare, your efforts will be rewarded with a memorable dish with most of the work done ahead. Before serving, the pasta squares are drizzled with *sugo di arrosto,* a reduced sauce that, in this case, is fragrant with the seductive essences of roasted meat, hearty red wine, caramelized vegetables, herbs, and tomatoes. This recipe makes more than the 1½ cups of filling needed for the tortellini. But it's so delicious, I think you will be tempted to taste it often as you prepare the pasta. The sauce will keep in the refrigerator for up to five days; uncooked filled tortellini can be frozen for up to two weeks. In all of my pasta recipes, I allow a little extra pasta in case you cut some of it incorrectly or it breaks as you fill it.

2 pounds oxtail pieces or short ribs, well trimmed and patted dry
with paper towels

Sea salt and freshly ground black pepper

¼ cup canola or vegetable oil

1 small yellow onion, chopped (½ cup)

1 small carrot, peeled and chopped (¼ cup)

1 small rib celery, trimmed and chopped (¼ cup)

One 14.5-ounce can peeled crushed tomatoes,
preferably from the San Marzano region

1 clove garlic, crushed

1 sprig fresh thyme

1 bay leaf

2 cups hearty red wine, such as Sangiovese or Barbera

2 cups Veal Stock (page 258) or Homemade Chicken Stock (page 255) or
   canned low-sodium stock

¼ cup freshly grated Parmigiano-Reggiano cheese, plus
   cheese for sprinkling

1 large egg, beaten

1 pound Basic Pasta (page 55), rolled out on
   thinnest setting, or store-bought pasta sheets

2 tablespoons unsalted butter

4 fresh sage leaves

Season the meat liberally with salt and pepper. In a large deep pot or Dutch oven, heat the oil over high heat until almost smoking. Add the oxtails in a single layer, always keeping the oil hot enough to sizzle as the pieces are added. Brown on all sides, 15 to 20 minutes, turning to color evenly. Remove the pieces with a slotted spoon and drain in a colander. Do this in batches, if necessary, so the pieces are not crowded.

Meanwhile, preheat the oven to 400°F.

Discard all but 2 tablespoons of fat from the pot. Stir in the onion, carrot, and celery and cook over medium-high heat, stirring constantly, until lightly colored, 5 to 6 minutes. Add the tomatoes, garlic, thyme, and bay leaf, stirring to incorporate all the browned bits in the pot, and cook for 2 to 3 minutes longer. Pour in the red wine, bring to a boil, and cook for 20 minutes or until the liquid has reduced by half. Then stir in the stock.

Return the meat to the pot. Bring the liquid to a simmer, cover, and transfer the pot to the oven for 1½ to 2 hours, or until the meat is completely tender when pierced with a fork. With a slotted spoon, lift the pieces from the sauce and put them on a sheet pan to cool.

Using a slotted spoon, remove about ½ cup of the vegetables and tomatoes from the pan and set aside. Pour the remaining sauce through a fine strainer into a clean pan, pressing to extract as much liquid as possible. Skim off as much fat as possible. The sauce should be thick and rich.

Pick the meat off the bones, chop into small pieces, and put in a large bowl. Combine the meat with the cheese, add the egg, season with salt and pepper, and stir to blend.

Purée the reserved vegetables in a food processor and stir them into the meat mixture. Set aside. If making the sauce ahead, cover and refrigerate for up to 5 days.

On a lightly floured work surface, use a sharp knife or pizza cutter and ruler to trim the sheets of pasta into 6- x 18-inch rectangles. Cut each rectangle into twelve 3-inch squares. As you work with one sheet, cover the remaining pasta with a clean cloth or plastic. In the end, you should have 54 three-inch squares. Line a baking sheet with parchment and dust lightly with cornmeal or flour.

Spoon about ½ teaspoon of filling in the center of each square. Mist the pasta lightly with water, cover with another pasta square, and press the pasta with your fingertips to seal the filling inside, making sure to press out all of the air. Trim the edges with a zigzag pasta wheel. Transfer to the baking sheet and set aside in a cool, dry spot. Once the tortellini are filled, they may be refrigerated for up to 1 day. Or put them into large resealable plastic bags, squeeze out the excess air, and freeze immediately for up to 2 weeks.

Bring a large pot of salted water to a boil. Stir in the tortellini. After they rise to the surface, cook for 1 minute longer, then remove with a slotted spoon and transfer to a large bowl. Drain any water that accumulates at the bottom of the bowl.

Heat the butter in a large pot. Add the sage, cook for 1 minute, then add the tortellini to the pan and toss to coat. Divide the tortellini evenly among 8 large plates, drizzle with the sauce, sprinkle with additional cheese, and serve.

Tortelli di Robiola
Robiola Cheese-Filled Tortelli

[MAKES 4 SERVINGS]

T*ortelli* are large squares of pasta—about three times the size of tortellini—filled in this recipe with tangy, creamy fresh *robiola* cheese from Piemonte and tossed with a quick tomato sauce. The cheese tastes similar to aged ricotta cheese. If you cannot find *robiola* at your local market, substitute equal amounts of fresh goat cheese and whole milk ricotta.

1 pound *robiola* cheese (about 2 cups)

½ cup freshly grated Parmigiano-Reggiano cheese

Pinch of freshly grated nutmeg

Sea salt and freshly ground white pepper

1 pound Basic Pasta (page 55), rolled out to thinnest setting, or
   store-bought sheets of fresh pasta

¼ cup extra-virgin olive oil, plus extra for drizzling

2 cloves garlic, thinly sliced

¼ cup loosely packed basil leaves

One 26-ounce can diced Italian plum tomatoes, undrained

In a large bowl, combine the *robiola* cheese, Parmigiano-Reggiano cheese, and nutmeg. Season to taste with salt and pepper and stir until smooth. Set aside.

On a lightly floured work surface, use a sharp knife or pizza cutter and ruler to trim the pasta into a 6- x 18-inch rectangle. Cut the pasta into twelve 3-inch squares: First cut it in half horizontally, then cut it vertically into 3-inch strips to make 12 squares. Repeat with the second sheet.

Place 2 teaspoons of the *robiola* filling in the center of each square. Lightly brush the edges of each square with water and cover with another pasta square. Press the pasta with your fingertips to seal the ball of *robiola* inside, making sure to press out all of the air. Trim the edges with a zigzag pasta wheel and set on a parchment paper-lined baking sheet lightly dusted with flour or cornmeal. Continue with the remaining pasta and filling until all the squares are filled.

Bring a large pot of salted water to a boil. Add the *tortelli* and cook until they rise to the surface, 3 to 5 minutes, then cook for 1 minute longer or until the centers are cooked through and the pasta is al dente. Remove with a skimmer or slotted spoon to a large bowl. Once they are all removed, drain any water from the bowl.

In a large skillet, combine the olive oil, garlic, and basil and cook over medium heat, stirring, until the garlic is softened, about 1 minute. Add the tomatoes and cook, stirring occasionally, for another 8 minutes. Add the *tortelli* to the pan and toss to coat them evenly with the sauce. Divide the *tortelli* among 4 plates, drizzle with a little olive oil, and serve immediately.

Gnocchi con Funghi e Fave
Gnocchi with Morels and Fava Beans

Homemade gnocchi are so satisfying, I hope you will make your own at least once to serve with the light mushroom sauce and fava beans in this dish. (Otherwise, some decent gnocchi are sold at specialty food stores and markets.) Cooking potatoes in their skins preserves the starch that holds the gnocchi together. Passing the peeled potatoes through a ricer or food mill ensures that they will have a light texture and smooth mouth feel. Gnocchi can also be tossed with Fresh Tomato Sauce (page 18) or Basic Tomato Sauce (page 260) and garnished with a few basil leaves.

Gnocchi

1¼ pounds Idaho or other baking potatoes

1¾ cups all-purpose flour

2 large eggs, beaten

½ cup freshly grated Parmigiano-Reggiano cheese

2 teaspoons sea salt, or to taste

⅛ teaspoon white pepper

Pinch of freshly ground nutmeg

Morel Sauce

3 tablespoons extra-virgin olive oil

1 clove garlic, crushed

1 sprig fresh rosemary

1½ pounds fresh morels, stems trimmed, rinsed, patted with paper towels, and cut in half, or a combination of morels and wiped, trimmed, and thickly sliced cremini, shiitake, and porcini mushrooms

½ cup dry white wine, such as Trebbiano or Pinot Grigio

90

½ cup Rich Chicken Stock (page 256)

Sea salt and freshly ground black pepper

1 cup shelled and blanched fresh fava beans (2½ to 3 pounds beans, see page 58)

1 tablespoon chopped flat-leaf parsley

2 tablespoons unsalted butter

¼ cup freshly grated Parmigiano-Reggiano cheese

To make the Gnocchi:

Put the potatoes in a large pot of water and cover with cold water. Bring the water to a boil and cook until the potatoes are easily pierced with a knife, about 20 minutes, then drain. When cool enough to handle, peel the potatoes and pass them through a potato ricer onto a lightly floured work surface. Using a fork, spread them out into about a 6-inch square to cool.

Make a well in the center of the potatoes. Pour in the eggs, sprinkle on 1½ cups of the flour, the cheese, salt, pepper, and nutmeg. Using your hands or two pastry scrapers, and working from the outside edges, knead until the mixture is just evenly blended, adding flour by the ¼ cup, as needed, 3 to 4 minutes. Do not overmix or the gnocchi will become tough and gluey.

Lightly dust your hands and the dough with flour. Form the dough into a log about 4 inches in diameter and sprinkle with flour. With a knife or dough scraper divide the log into 6 equal pieces. Roll each piece into a cylinder about ½ inch in diameter. Cut into 1-inch pieces, put on a tray lined with waxed paper and dusted with flour, and set aside.

To make the Morel Sauce:

In a large skillet, heat the olive oil over medium-high heat. Add the garlic and rosemary and cook, stirring, until the oil is very fragrant, 1 to 2 minutes. Add the mushrooms and cook, tossing gently to color them on all sides, for 2 to 3 minutes. Pour the white wine over the mushrooms, stir up all the browned bits, and continue cooking until the wine evaporates, about 3 minutes. Add the chicken stock, stir in the beans, and simmer over low heat until the beans are almost tender, 3 to 5 minutes. Season to taste with salt and pepper and keep warm.

Bring a very large pot of salted water to a boil. Add the gnocchi and, when the water returns to a boil, cook until they rise to the surface, 2 to 3 minutes, then cook for an additional 30 to 40 seconds, until tender. Remove the gnocchi to a large bowl with a slotted spoon and drain well. Add the gnocchi, parsley, and butter to the skillet with the sauce and toss until the gnocchi are well coated. Remove the pan from the heat, discard the rosemary sprig, sprinkle with Parmigiano-Reggiano, and divide the gnocchi among 4 large plates. Serve immediately.

Morbidelle con Fonduta al Formaggio
Robiola Cheese with Soft Polenta and Fonduta

[MAKES 4 SERVINGS]

In Italian, *morbido* means soft or creamy. And while each component of this decadently rich dish is soft, there is a seductive play of textures and temperatures in each bite. A cool ball of smooth *robiola Piemonte* cheese (page 88) is covered by soft, slightly grainy polenta. Then the silky hot *fonduta*—an orgasmic white truffle-laced fontina cheese sauce—is ladled on. The two layers hide the cheese ball and begin to warm it. The combination of flavors and textures entice you to take bite after bite until not one morsel is left. As for how many white truffles to shave on top, what can I say? This is a good place to splurge! The truffles really do make this dish.

8 ounces (1 cup) *robiola* cheese, or substitute equal parts
   whole milk ricotta and cream cheese

½ cup fresh goat cheese, softened

2 tablespoons truffle oil or white truffle paste (see Sources, page 266)

Sea salt

1 cup coarse yellow cornmeal or instant polenta

Freshly ground black pepper

1½ cups heavy cream

8 ounces fontina cheese, cut into chunks

6 large egg yolks

¾ ounce white truffles, shaved

2 teaspoons soft unsalted butter, if cooking fontina cheese sauce ahead

In a medium-size bowl, blend the *robiola* and goat cheeses with 1 tablespoon of the truffle oil or paste until smooth. Roll the mixture into 4 equal balls and refrigerate while preparing the remaining ingredients.

In a large saucepan, add a teaspoon of salt and bring 3 cups water to a boil. Slowly add the cornmeal in a thin stream, whisking with a wooden spoon to prevent lumps. Continue to simmer for 1 hour, stirring continuously, until the cornmeal is smooth and satiny on the tongue (see page 54). Season to taste with salt and pepper. (For instant polenta, cook according to the package instructions.)

Heat the cream and fontina in a heavy saucepan over medium heat until the cheese is melted. Off the heat, whisk in the egg yolks, beating constantly, then return the pan to medium heat and continue whisking until the mixture thickens, 4 to 6 minutes. Stir in the remaining 1 tablespoon of truffle oil or paste and keep warm over a low heat.

If cooking the fontina cheese sauce ahead, put 2 teaspoons unsalted butter on the surface. The melted butter will prevent a skin from forming. Set the sauce over a pan of simmering water.

Place each ball of *robiola* in a soup bowl. Ladle on the hot polenta, pour the *fonduta* over this, top with shaved white truffles, if using, and serve.

Polenta con Rape e Pancetta
Baked Polenta with Sautéed Broccoli Rabe and Pancetta

[MAKES 6 APPETIZER SERVINGS]

Oven-baked polenta cut into squares or circles and topped with broccoli rabe scented with pancetta and a touch of Pecorino Romano cheese make a tasty appetizer. As a variation, try caponata (page 117) or bits of the braised short ribs (page 172) on them. Once the polenta is cooked and poured into the sheet pan, it and the cooked broccoli rabe may be refrigerated overnight.

2 cups Homemade Chicken Stock (page 255) or canned low-sodium stock

Sea salt

1⅓ cups coarse yellow cornmeal (about 7 ounces), or substitute instant polenta

¼ cup extra-virgin olive oil

6 ounces thickly sliced pancetta, cut into ¼-inch cubes (about 1¼ cups)

1 large yellow onion, thinly sliced (1¼ cups)

2 large garlic cloves, thinly sliced

½ teaspoon red pepper flakes

2 pounds broccoli rabe, thick stems removed and discarded, cut into 3-inch lengths

Freshly ground black pepper

½ cup freshly grated Pecorino Romano cheese

Preheat the oven to 425°F. Lightly oil an 8- x 11½-inch or 9- x 13-inch baking dish.

In a medium-size saucepan, bring the chicken stock and 2 cups water to a boil. Add 1 teaspoon salt and gradually whisk in the cornmeal until smooth. Cook over medium heat, stirring with a wooden spoon, until it has thickened, about 10 minutes. Pour the polenta into the oiled baking dish and smooth the top; brush the top with 1 tablespoon of the olive oil. Bake for 1 hour 15 minutes or until the top and bottom are golden and crusty.

Meanwhile, in a large deep skillet, heat the remaining 3 tablespoons of olive oil over medium-high heat until hot but not smoking. Stir in the pancetta and cook until golden, 4 to 5 minutes, stirring frequently. Add the onion, garlic, and pepper flakes and cook, stirring, until the onion softens, 5 to 6 minutes. Add the broccoli rabe and 1/4 cup water, season to taste with salt and pepper, and toss gently. Cover and cook until the broccoli rabe is softened, about 5 minutes. Uncover and cook, stirring occasionally, until the water has evaporated and the broccoli rabe is completely tender, 2 minutes longer.

Cut the polenta into 6 equal pieces and transfer them to 6 small plates or, using a small circular cutter, cut the polenta into circles. Stir 1/4 cup of the Pecorino into the broccoli rabe and spoon it over the polenta. Sprinkle with the remaining 1/4 cup of the Pecorino and serve.

Risotto alla Pescatora
Fisherman's Risotto

[MAKES 4 MAIN COURSE SERVINGS]

Seaside villages along Italy's Adriatic coast are filled with charming trattorias where simple yet robust dishes, like this colorful seafood risotto, typically showcase the catch of the day. Once the risotto is cooked, the fisherman-style sauce takes just minutes to complete. Serve the creamy rice in a large flat bowl with the sauce generously ladled on top. As with other seafood risottos prepared in Italy, I don't serve grated cheese with this one.

Risotto

1 tablespoon extra-virgin olive oil, plus 2 or 3 tablespoons additional oil to finish the risotto

1 tablespoon unsalted butter

1 small yellow onion, peeled and chopped (½ cup)

2 cups Arborio rice

1 cup dry white wine, such as Pinot Grigio or Sauvignon Blanc

4 to 5 cups Homemade Chicken Stock (page 255) or canned low-sodium stock, heated

Pescatore Sauce

2 tablespoons extra-virgin olive oil, plus extra for drizzling

2 large cloves garlic, crushed

½ pound Manila, littleneck, or cherrystone clams, scrubbed and purged (see page 122)

½ pound mussels, scrubbed and debearded

½ pound large shrimp, peeled and deveined

continued

¼ cup squid (bodies only), cleaned, split lengthwise, and cut
crosswise into thin slices

1 cup dry white wine, such as Pinot Grigio or Sauvignon Blanc

2 tablespoons finely chopped flat-leaf parsley plus additional for sprinkling

Pinch of red pepper flakes

Sea salt and freshly ground black pepper

½ cup grape tomatoes, cut in half

To make the Risotto:

In a large heavy skillet or saucepan, heat 1 tablespoon of the olive oil and the butter over medium-high heat until hot. Stir in the onion and cook until it is soft and translucent, 4 to 5 minutes. Add the rice, stirring to coat thoroughly with the oil, and cook for 3 to 4 minutes until the grains look opaque. Pour in the wine and cook it over high heat until the liquid almost completely evaporates, stirring constantly.

Adjust the heat down to medium-low. Slowly add the heated stock—about ½ cup at a time—so that the rice stays wet but is never completely covered with liquid. Stir continuously. Once the rice absorbs all of the first amount of stock, continue adding ½ cupfuls of stock, letting each be absorbed before continuing with the next, and stirring constantly. Be patient and keep the heat on gentle. You should see the steam when you add the stock, but the rice should not stick.

Continue cooking until the rice is tender but still has a tiny hard spot in the center, 17 to 19 minutes of simmering time. The amount of liquid to be added can vary, but you should reserve ⅓ cup of stock to loosen the risotto before serving.

Have ready 4 heated flat bowls. Once the risotto is al dente, remove the pan from the heat and stir in 2 tablespoons of the remaining extra-virgin olive oil and the final ⅓ cup of stock. Tent the pan with aluminum foil and keep it warm over very low heat until ready to prepare the sauce, then ladle the risotto into the bowls, shaking or tapping each dish to spread it evenly in the bottom.

To make the Pescatore Sauce:

In a large deep skillet or saucepan, heat the olive oil over medium-high heat until hot. Add the garlic and cook, stirring, until lightly colored, about 2 minutes. Add the clams, mussels, shrimp, and squid, cover, and cook until the shrimp are pink and cooked, and the clams and mussels have opened, 5 to 6 minutes. Discard any shellfish that do not open. Using a slotted spoon, spoon the shellfish onto the risotto.

Pour the wine into the pan and add the tomatoes, parsley, and red pepper flakes. Bring the liquid to a boil over high heat and cook, mashing the tomatoes a bit with the back of a wooden spoon, until reduced by half, 1 to 2 minutes. Season to taste with salt and pepper. Ladle the reduced broth over the shellfish and risotto. Top with a little parsley and a final drizzle of extra-virgin olive oil and serve immediately.

pesce

Carpaccio di Branzino con Finnochio, Pomodori e Olive Wild Striped Sea Bass Carpaccio with Fennel, Tomatoes, and Ligurian Olives Branzino in Acqua Pazza Sea Bass in "Crazy Water" Branzino con Salsa di Salmoriglio Sea Bass with Salmoriglio Sauce San Pietro con Carciofi e Basilico John Dory with Artichokes and Basil Ipoglosso con Couscous Halibut with Couscous Tonno con Caponata Tuna with Caponata Merluzzo con Frutti di Mare Cod with Shellfish Pesce Spada alla Griglia con Caponata di Carciofi Grilled Swordfish with Artichoke Caponata Astice alla Griglia con Pesto al Limone Grilled Lobster with Citrus Pesto Sauce Salmone in Padella con Prugne, Pesche e Pomodori Pan-Roasted Salmon with Black Plums, Peaches, and Tomatoes Dentice al Rosmarino con Cicoria e Fagioli Roasted Red Snapper with Chicory and White Beans Zuppa di Pesce Fish Soup

FISH

The Italian peninsula is surrounded by water: the Ligurian, Tyrrhenian, and Mediterranean Seas to the west; the Ionian Sea to the south; and the Adriatic to the east. There are numerous inland lakes and rivers, as well, so sources for fresh fish and shellfish are never far away.

During my years in Italy, I ate seafood everywhere and came to love it. It was never fancy but always very satisfying. It gave me—a guy from Wisconsin who grew up on lake fish and not even very much of that—a newfound respect and understanding of how delicious fish can be without the flavors being masked. Although the varieties of fish in America may be different, the lessons I learned in Italy about careful selection and proper preparation apply anywhere.

Italians use fish and shellfish liberally in hot and cold antipasti. The succulent grilled octopus with gigante beans on page 14 is just one simple but satisfying example. Pasta and risotto dishes similar to those in the previous chapter are other tasty possibilities. In this chapter, my passion for main course seafood dishes takes center stage, from simple grilled preparations to a hearty fish soup.

Italians relish seafood, but they are also finicky eaters and insist upon freshness. When I worked at the two-starred restaurant San Domenico in Imola, the boats came in on Wednesday, Friday, and Saturday. If there was no branzino, for example, we went on to our next choice and used the fish as fast as it arrived.

I learned that beyond exquisite freshness, invariably what characterizes Italian seafood is the simplicity of its preparation. In seaside trattorias, freshly caught fish and shellfish is grilled and seasoned with just an herb or two and salt and pepper. The Grilled Lobster with Citrus Pesto Sauce on page 125 is just such a preparation. It is the essence of summertime dining at its best.

A small plate of vegetables or potatoes may accompany the dish. But the fish itself will probably be dressed with nothing more than a squeeze of fresh lemon juice or light vinaigrette. *Salmoriglio* (page 109) is a ubiquitous sauce made with olive oil, lemon juice, and herbs that you find on many restaurant tables. If you are like me, after one taste, you will begin to spoon this condiment over every fish and even grilled chicken dish imaginable.

In the addition to the grill, some fish are pan roasted or baked. Most often, they are cooked whole, on the bone, because the meat remains juicier and the pieces are less likely to fall apart when filleted and served. I have given you directions for filleting red snapper in the hope that you will attempt to learn this simple skill.

Fish in Italy are also simmered in simple broths. The most elemental example of this is Neapolitan-style fish in "crazy water." While at sea, local fishermen cook a fish or two in a little brazier or metal pan of hot ocean water seasoned with herbs and pepper. My version of crazy water (page 107) is true to that spirit, but I elevate the basic preparation with an enriched broth and some aromatic vegetables along with sea bass and shrimp.

There are fish soups made with just a few ingredients and others that combine several different kinds of seafood. Even in those that are well seasoned with plenty of garlic, tomatoes, wine, or other flavorings, nothing is added gratuitously, so each ingredient retains its distinct taste.

While Italians have a rich culinary tradition, over the centuries some foreign ingredients have made their way into Italian kitchens. Early on, tomatoes came from the New World via ship. More recently, modern transportation has expanded the market. Salmon—which is not indigenous to Italy—is now imported and becoming more popular.

I like the notion of combining old and new, local and imported. It is the genesis for several of my dishes that are Italian in style or spirit but made with locally grown American provisions. One is a beautiful square of opalescent halibut, a favorite fish among American diners but unavailable in Italy. It is steamed and served on a mound of couscous scented with saffron, almonds, and currants (page 115).

Another, Tuna with Caponata (page 117), is among our most popular fish offerings. Caponata is a centuries-old Sicilian dish most frequently made with eggplant or, as I do here, with artichokes. Pairing beautiful slices of rare tuna with the tangy vegetable mixture creates an exciting contrast of tastes, temperatures, and textures. Similarly, salmon in Italy might be served as I cook it at Fiamma: pan-broiled or grilled. I add a bright, modern fruit salsa (page 128).

Many of the fish and shellfish found in Italy do not exist here. Rather than bemoaning that, I have taken the best of what is available here and used the same simple preparations I learned in Italy. Following a few guidelines, there are some excellent choices. First, get to know the person at the store where you buy fish. Find out when they receive fresh orders. If a piece of fish smells fishy, forget it; it isn't fresh. At home, quickly use whichever fish or shellfish you buy. Take a tip from the Italians: cook it within a day or two at the most.

Hopefully the recipes in this and other chapters will inspire you to cook fish more often. As you will discover, these dishes really are quite simple to prepare. Beyond their simplicity, they leave you with a feeling of well-being, as if you have dined on something lighter and, perhaps, more sophisticated.

Carpaccio di Branzino con Finnochio, Pomodori e Olive
Wild Striped Sea Bass Carpaccio with Fennel, Tomatoes, and Ligurian Olives

[MAKES 4 SERVINGS]

Carpaccio of sea bass with fennel, tomatoes, and Ligurian olives is the epitome of a clean-tasting fresh dish that is almost instantly prepared. Southern Italians eat a lot of raw fish, especially during the sweltering summer months when simple, direct foods are favored. In any dish where raw fish is used, it is essential to buy from a reliable fishmonger, where the turnover is high, and carefully select the best fish and accompaniments available. The dish may be assembled up to an hour ahead of time and left at room temperature.

2 large ripe, flavorful tomatoes, such as beefsteak

1 small bulb fennel

¾ cup extra-virgin olive oil

2 tablespoons freshly squeezed lemon juice

1 teaspoon fresh thyme leaves

1 shallot, minced

Sea salt and freshly ground black pepper

12 ounces wild striped sea bass

3 cups lightly packed arugula leaves

½ cup mild black olives, preferably Ligurian, pitted and roughly chopped

Core the tomatoes and cut a small "x" in each base. Fill a pot three-quarters full of water and bring to a boil. Add the tomatoes and cook until the skin begins to peel away from the base, about 1 minute. Remove with a slotted spoon and set aside until they are cool enough to handle. Using a sharp paring knife, peel off the skin. (If it doesn't come off easily, return the tomatoes to boiling water for 10 to 20 seconds longer, depending on how ripe they are.)

Slice the tomatoes in half crosswise. Holding each half in the palm of your hand, gently squeeze out the seeds and discard. Dice the tomatoes and set aside.

Trim the fronds and stalks from the fennel. Cut the bulb in half lengthwise, remove the core, and then cut it crosswise into very thin slices with a mandoline or sharp knife. Set aside.

Whisk together the olive oil, lemon juice, thyme, and shallot in a small bowl. Season to taste with salt and pepper and set aside.

Using a very sharp slicing knife, cut the fish across the grain into 28 paper-thin slices. Divide the sea bass among 4 salad plates, overlapping the slices in the center of the plate. Lay the arugula leaves around the outside of the plates, then spoon the tomatoes, fennel, and olives around the fish. Drizzle the vinaigrette over the fish and vegetables and serve.

Taggiasca Olives from Liguria

The black olives I use in this recipe are named for Taggia, a town in western Liguria along the Italian Rivera. Benedictine monks first developed this variety of olive thousands of years ago. The small, low-acid olives are now found all the way north to Monaco and are appearing in American specialty food stores as well. Similar to but somewhat larger than French niçoise olives, the delicate sweet-flavored olives are both eaten and used for their oil. When pressed early in the season, the oil is somewhat peppery; it softens and becomes fruitier as the olives mature.

Branzino in Acqua Pazza
Sea Bass in "Crazy Water"

[MAKES 4 SERVINGS]

Fisherman around Naples are known to throw their first catch of the day into a little brazier, or metal pot, set over burning coals or charcoal on board their boats. They cook the fish in "crazy water," or seawater seasoned with pepper and spices. My version of this simple fisherman's stew elevates the dish to a slightly more sophisticated level by poaching the fish in broth and serving it on garlic-rubbed crostini.

Neapolitans are known for their love of garlic and this dish has plenty, so decide on the amount that suits you. I suggest using fresh tomatoes in the stew because you want a light, drinkable broth for the fish. Canned tomatoes will make the liquid cloudy. For the broth, buy unpeeled shrimp and reserve the shells. Or ask your seafood store to save the bones of non-oily white fish for the stock.

4 large ripe tomatoes

16 large shrimp

4 tablespoons extra-virgin olive oil

4 to 6 cloves garlic, crushed, plus extra for rubbing

1 medium-large yellow onion, coarsely chopped (1 cup)

2 tablespoons tomato paste

1/4 teaspoon red pepper flakes

Sea salt

Four 7-ounce sea bass fillets

Four 1/2-inch-thick slices rustic Italian bread, about 6 inches in diameter

Lemon Olive Oil (optional; page 253), or additional olive oil
    with a few drops of lemon juice added, for drizzling

Core the tomatoes and cut a small "x" in each base. Fill a large pot three-quarters full of water and bring to a boil. Add the tomatoes and cook until the skin begins to peel away from the base, about 1 minute. Remove with a slotted spoon and set aside until they are cool enough to handle. Using a sharp paring knife, peel off the skin. (If it doesn't come off easily, return the tomatoes to boiling water for 10 to 20 seconds longer, depending on how ripe they are.)

Slice the tomatoes in half crosswise. Holding each half in the palm of your hand, gently squeeze out the seeds and discard. Dice the tomatoes and set aside. You should have about 4 cups of diced tomatoes.

Peel and devein the shrimp, reserving the shells. Set the shrimp aside.

Heat 2 tablespoons of the olive oil in a large, deep casserole over medium heat. Add 2 to 4 cloves of garlic, according to taste, and cook, stirring, for 2 to 3 minutes. Stir in the shrimp shells, onion, and 2 cups of the tomatoes. Reduce the heat and simmer until the shells are very soft, 45 minutes to 1 hour. Stir in the tomato paste, pepper flakes, and a pinch of salt. Add enough water to cover and simmer for 1 hour longer. Pour the liquid through a fine strainer, discard the solids, and set the broth aside.

Heat the remaining 2 tablespoons of the olive oil in a large, deep skillet over medium heat. Add the remaining 2 cloves of garlic and cook for 2 minutes, stirring constantly. Stir in the fish broth and add the remaining tomatoes. Lay the sea bass on top of the broth and poach for 3 to 4 minutes. Add the shrimp and continue cooking until the fillets are just opaque and the shrimp are cooked through, 6 to 7 minutes total cooking time.

Meanwhile, lightly toast the bread, then rub each slice with garlic. Put the toasted bread in 4 warmed flat soup bowls. Using a wide spatula, place a fillet on each slice, divide the shrimp evenly, spoon the broth over the fish, drizzle with a little Lemon Oil, if desired, and serve.

Branzino con Salsa di Salmoriglio
Sea Bass with Salmoriglio Sauce

[MAKES 2 SERVINGS]

Salmoriglio is a warm sauce made with olive oil, lemon juice, and herbs whisked together into a vinaigrette-like condiment. It is a legacy of Sicilian cooking. Purists say you should only beat in seawater, but most people use tap water. You can serve it with many dishes, including this grilled sea bass, other fish dishes, cold chicken, and roast beef. I use fresh flat-leaf parsley with dried oregano in my version—but there are many variations of the sauce. Some cooks use fresh oregano with parsley, others add crushed tomatoes, and many replace lemon with vinegar. You can make the sauce in advance and keep it in the refrigerator in a covered container for at least a week. Stir it before using.

Salmoriglio Sauce

½ cup extra-virgin olive oil

Juice of 2 lemons

Sea salt

1 clove garlic, minced

2 teaspoons dried oregano

2 tablespoons chopped flat-leaf parsley leaves

Freshly ground black pepper

Sea Bass

Two 1½-pound whole sea bass, scaled and gutted

Olive oil

Sea salt and freshly ground black pepper

1 large lemon, cut into thin slices

2 to 3 sprigs fresh rosemary

2 to 3 sprigs flat-leaf parsley

To make the Salmoriglio Sauce:

Partially fill the bottom of a double boiler with water and bring to a boil. The water should not touch the top insert. Pour the olive oil into the insert and, using a small whisk, gradually beat in ½ cup hot water and the lemon juice. Cook for 5 minutes, beating continuously, until the sauce is slightly thickened; it will not emulsify. Stir in the salt, garlic, oregano, parsley, and black pepper to taste; keep warm while cooking the fish.

To cook the Sea Bass:

Heat a gas or charcoal grill to medium-high heat. Position the grates about 4 inches from the heat. The coals should have a medium glow but should not be too hot. Brush the fish on both sides with olive oil and season with salt and pepper. Fill the cavities with the lemon slices, rosemary, and parsley.

Place the fish on the grill and cook for 6 to 7 minutes on one side, turn, and cook on the second side until the meat flakes easily with a fork and appears opaque all the way through, 6 to 7 minutes more. Remove the fish from the grill and fillet them (see page 132). (Alternatively, broil them under a preheated broiler 4 inches from the heat for 6 to 7 minutes per side.) Transfer the fillets to 2 large plates, drizzle with *Salmoriglio* Sauce, and serve. Pass extra sauce at the table.

San Pietro con Carciofi e Basilico
John Dory with Artichokes and Basil

[MAKES 6 SERVINGS]

San Pietro fish, also known as John Dory, is a saltwater fish with firm, white flesh similar to sole. It is part of the tilapia family. It is usually cut into fillets, as in this dish, where it is served on a tasty ragout of artichokes, fennel, and aromatic vegetables. I think of the fish as subtle and sexy. To maintain that appeal, it should be cooked gently until just done. The fish's name in Italian comes from the two dark spots on its sides, said to be the fingerprints of Saint Peter.

½ small bulb fennel

4 tablespoons extra-virgin olive oil, plus extra for drizzling

4 artichoke hearts, cut into eighths (see page 69)

1 small yellow onion, sliced (about ½ cup)

1 large carrot, peeled and diced (½ cup)

2 garlic cloves, crushed

1 cup Fish Stock (page 254)

½ cup dry white wine, such as Pinot Grigio

6 skinless John Dory fillets, about 6 ounces each, patted dry with paper towels

Sea salt and freshly ground black pepper

½ cup grape tomatoes, cut in half

¼ cup torn fresh basil leaves, plus extra leaves for garnish

1 teaspoon red pepper flakes

Juice of ½ lemon

Trim the fronds and stalks from the fennel. Remove the core and cut crosswise into thin slices.

Heat 2 tablespoons of the olive oil in a large skillet over medium-high heat. Add the artichokes, onion, carrot, fennel, and garlic and cook, stirring, until the vegetables begin to soften, about 5 minutes. Pour in the fish stock and wine, stir up any browned bits, and bring the liquid to a boil over high heat. Reduce the heat so the liquid is simmering and cook until the vegetables are fork tender, 25 to 30 minutes.

When the vegetables are almost cooked through, season the fish with salt and pepper. Heat the remaining 2 tablespoons of the olive oil in a large skillet over medium heat until hot. Lay the fillets in the pan, flesh side down, and gently cook for about 3 minutes. Using a wide spatula, turn the fillets over and cook until the fish is just cooked through and no longer translucent, about 2 minutes more; it should be firm to the touch.

After turning the fish fillets, gently stir in the tomatoes, basil, pepper flakes, and lemon juice so as not to break the fillets and cook just to heat through, about 1 minute. Season the mixture to taste with salt and pepper. Ladle the vegetable stew into 4 wide soup bowls. Transfer the fillets to the bowls, add a drizzle of olive oil and a few basil leaves to garnish, and serve.

Ipoglosso con Couscous
Halibut with Couscous

This seafood dish reflects the Arab influence in southern Italian cooking. Although there isn't any halibut in Sicily, I think the pearly white, mild fish is a nice partner for couscous scented with raisins, saffron, and slivered almonds. This tasty dish is easily and quickly prepared. You can even cook the couscous ahead and reheat it in a microwave for 3 to 4 minutes in a covered dish.

¼ cup slivered almonds or shelled pistachio nuts

1 cup uncooked couscous

1 stick cinnamon

Pinch of saffron threads

4 cups Fish Stock (page 254)

2 teaspoons Lemon Olive Oil (page 253) or olive oil with a few drops of lemon juice added, plus extra oil for garnish

½ cup golden raisins or currants

Sea salt and freshly ground black pepper

Four 7-ounce skinless halibut fillets

12 jumbo shrimp, peeled and deveined

2 tablespoons extra-virgin olive oil

2 cloves garlic, crushed

1½ pounds farmed mussels, scrubbed and debearded

4 ounces squid bodies, split lengthwise and cut into thin strips

2 tablespoons julienned or chopped flat-leaf parsley

Preheat the oven to 400°F. Spread the nuts on a sheet pan and bake until golden brown, 5 to 6 minutes, shaking the pan once or twice, and watching carefully that they do not burn. Remove and set aside.

Combine the couscous, cinnamon, and saffron in a large bowl. Bring 2 cups of the stock to a boil. Pour it over the couscous, cover tightly, and set the bowl in a warm spot, such as the back of the stove, but not over a flame. After 5 minutes, fluff the couscous with a fork and let it stand until all the liquid has been absorbed. Stir in the Lemon Olive Oil, raisins, and almonds, season to taste with salt and pepper, cover, and keep warm.

Season the halibut and shrimp with salt and pepper. Heat the olive oil in a large skillet over medium-high heat. Add the garlic and cook, stirring, until softened, about 2 minutes. Add the halibut, shrimp, and mussels and shake the pan. Pour in the remaining 2 cups of Fish Stock, cover, and steam for 2 minutes. Add the squid and continue cooking until the halibut is just cooked through, 1 to 2 minutes longer, to ensure that the squid remains tender. Remove the fish and shellfish with a slotted spoon and set aside. Discard any mussels that don't open.

Make a mound of the couscous in the center of each of 4 large plates. Lay the halibut on the couscous, then divide the shellfish among the plates. Sprinkle a little parsley on top, ladle 3 to 4 tablespoons of the poaching liquid over the fish, add a few drops of Lemon Olive Oil or olive oil, and serve at once.

Tonno con Caponata
Tuna with Caponata

[MAKES 6 SERVINGS]

Caponata is a centuries-old
Sicilian antipasto or side dish, typically made with eggplant and served at room temperature.
It reflects the Arab or Moorish influence on southern Italian cooking, since eggplants are said to have
originated in Asia before being introduced to Italy by thirteenth-century Arab traders.
In caponata, fried vegetable cubes are blended with raisins and spices in a sweet and sour liquid.
Combining caponata with rare seared tuna represents the melding of time-honored and contemporary
elements of Italian cooking today. Tuna is easy to overcook, so watch the timing carefully.

2 tablespoons fennel seeds

2 tablespoons coriander seeds

2 tablespoons yellow mustard seeds

2 to 3 cups canola oil, for deep-frying

3 red bell peppers, seeds and membranes removed, cut into ½-inch cubes

2 large unpeeled eggplants, cut into ¾-inch cubes

1 cup white wine vinegar

½ cup sugar

1 medium-large yellow onion, diced (1 cup)

1 large rib celery, trimmed and diced (½ cup)

½ cup golden raisins

3 oil-packed anchovy fillets, rinsed and blotted on paper towels

½ cup loosely packed, julienned fresh basil leaves, plus a few leaves for garnish

Sea salt and freshly ground black pepper

continued

117

Six 6- to 7-ounce tuna steaks, about 1 inch thick, blotted dry with paper towels

2 tablespoons extra-virgin olive oil, plus extra for drizzling

Coarse sea salt

Saba for drizzling (optional; see sidebar)

Heat the fennel, coriander, and mustard seeds in a skillet over medium heat, shaking the pan frequently, until fragrant, 2 to 3 minutes. Remove and, when cool, grind into a powder in a clean coffee grinder. Set aside.

Heat a deep-fat fryer or fill a deep pot with oil and heat to 375°F. Add the peppers and eggplant and cook over high heat until the eggplant is golden brown and crisp but soft in the center, 6 to 7 minutes. Remove the vegetables with a slotted spoon, drain on paper towels, and transfer to a large bowl.

Combine the vinegar, sugar, onion, celery, raisins, and anchovies in a nonreactive skillet. Bring to a boil over medium heat and cook, stirring occasionally, until the sugar melts and the liquid has reduced by half, 10 to 12 minutes. Scrape into the bowl with the vegetables and toss gently. Season to taste with salt and pepper. Once the caponata cools, add the basil and toss to blend.

Rub the spice mixture onto the tuna steaks. Heat the olive oil in a large heavy skillet over high heat until hot. Add the tuna and cook for 2 minutes on one side for rare, then turn and cook the second side for 2 minutes. (Cook 3 to 4 minutes per side for medium-rare.) Remove the tuna from the pan, set it on a plate, and let rest for 2 minutes.

Using about ¾ cup of caponata for each serving, make an oval mound in the center of each of 4 large plates. Cut the tuna across the grain into ¾-inch slices and lay them over the caponata. Sprinkle on a little coarse sea salt and drizzle with a little *saba*, if desired. Garnish with a basil leaf and serve.

Saba

Saba is a magical ingredient produced in Emilia-Romagna. It is made by boiling the must—the juice, pulp, skins, stems, and seeds—of freshly pressed Trebbiano grapes, the same grapes used for balsamic vinegar, down to the texture of maple syrup. Before sugar was generally available in Italy, *saba* was often the source of sweetness. It adds pizzazz to many dishes. Typically, it is drizzled on a piece of cheese or over gelato. It is delicious spooned over ice cream, cakes, or even dripped onto salads. Saba is also used as an elixir to settle the stomach; a teaspoon is poured into a glass and sparkling water is added.

You can find *saba* at some specialty food stores or on the Internet from Zingerman's (see Sources, page 266). While not the same as *saba*, balsamic vinegar cooked until reduced by two-thirds to a sweet-tangy syrup may be substituted in recipes.

Merluzzo con Frutti di Mare
Cod with Shellfish

[MAKES 4 SERVINGS]

Cod is an especially popular fish in the United States, largely because of its delicate, nonassertive taste. It can be served with mild or fairly aggressively flavored ingredients. In this light main course, clams and mussels garnish the fillets. The straightforward dish is served in a simple tomato-based broth. A well-seasoned mayonnaise or Salmoriglio Sauce (page 109) would also be an appropriate condiment for the cod. Mediterranean cooks often salt the fish and dry it for *baccalà* (as it is known in Italian).

4 tablespoons extra-virgin olive oil, plus extra for drizzling

1 large yellow onion, diced (1¼ cups)

4 cloves garlic, thinly sliced

2 cups small cherry or grape tomatoes, cut in half

Generous pinch of red pepper flakes, or to taste

1 pound mussels, scrubbed and debearded

1 pound small Manila, littleneck, or cherrystone clams, scrubbed and purged (see sidebar)

1½ cups dry white wine, such as Pinot Grigio

Four 7-ounce cod fillets, skin left on

Sea salt and freshly ground black pepper

1 tablespoon chopped basil

Preheat the oven to 375°F.

In a large deep skillet, heat the olive oil over medium heat. Add the onion and garlic and cook, stirring, until transparent, about 3 minutes. Stir in the tomatoes and pepper flakes and cook, stirring, for 2 to 3 minutes. Add the mussels, clams, and wine, cover the pan, reduce the heat so the liquid is just simmering, and cook for 6 minutes.

Season the cod fillets with salt and pepper. Push the clams and mussels to the side of the pan. Lay

the fillets in the pan on top of the tomatoes. Cover the pan, return the liquid to a boil, then transfer the pan to the oven to cook until the cod is cooked through, 6 to 7 minutes. Remove the pan from the oven and let stand for 2 to 3 minutes.

Discard any shellfish that do not open. Place one fillet on each plate. Divide the shellfish evenly among the plates, ladling it around each fillet. Sprinkle with a little basil, drizzle with olive oil, and serve.

Purging Clams

Purging clams helps to remove the sandy contents from their stomachs. Soak them in cold, lightly salted water for at least 15 to 20 minutes, changing the water a couple of times, then rinse before using.

Pesce Spada alla Griglia con Caponata di Carciofi
Grilled Swordfish with Artichoke Caponata

[MAKES 4 SERVINGS]

Americans typically know of caponata as a condiment made with eggplants. While that is the most familiar version (see page 117), a delightful variation is prepared with artichokes. Here it makes a tasty topping for swordfish, but you can serve it with many grilled foods, including chicken breasts, rabbit, turkey cutlets, and salmon.

Juice of 1 lemon

8 fresh artichoke hearts, with about 1½ inches of stem left on, leaves and chokes removed (see page 69)

5 tablespoons extra-virgin olive oil

1 medium yellow onion, diced (¾ cup)

3 cloves garlic, sliced

4 ribs celery, trimmed with leaves and strings removed, diced (1½ cups)

½ cup canned crushed tomatoes

½ cup dry white wine, such as Trebbiano or Pinot Grigio

¼ cup white wine vinegar

3 to 4 tablespoons sugar

¼ cup pine nuts

2 tablespoons small capers, drained

Sea salt and freshly ground black pepper

continued

½ cup Cerignola or other large green imported olives,
   pitted and coarsely chopped

3 tablespoons julienned fresh basil leaves

Saba (optional; see page 118)

Four 7-ounce swordfish steaks, about 1-inch thick

Add the lemon juice to a large bowl of water. Cut the artichoke hearts perpendicular to the flat surface of the heart into thick slices, and drop them in the acidulated water to keep from darkening.

In a large nonreactive skillet, heat 4 tablespoons of the olive oil over medium-high heat. Add the onion and garlic and cook, stirring, over medium heat until the onion is wilted, 3 to 4 minutes. Add the artichokes and celery and cook, stirring, until they begin to color, 3 to 4 minutes more. Stir in the crushed tomatoes, wine, vinegar, 3 tablespoons of the sugar, the pine nuts, and capers. Season to taste with salt and pepper. Cook over medium heat, stirring occasionally, until the artichokes are fork tender, 20 to 25 minutes. Remove the pan from the stove, taste to adjust the seasonings, and add more sugar if the mixture is too acidic. Stir in the olives and basil and let the caponata cool.

Heat a gas or charcoal indoor or outdoor grill until medium-hot. Position the grates about 4 inches from the heat. Brush the swordfish steaks with a little of the remaining oil, season with salt and pepper, lay them on the grates, and cook the first side for 4 to 5 minutes. Turn and cook the second side until the fish is firm to the touch, 4 to 5 minutes more. (Alternatively, broil them under a preheated broiler, with the pan 4 inches from the heat, for 4 to 5 minutes per side.)

Remove the fish and let it stand for 5 minutes. Serve each swordfish steak with a large spoonful of artichoke caponata in the middle. Lightly drizzle with *saba*, if desired, and serve.

Astice Alla Griglia con Pesto al Limone
Grilled Lobster with Citrus Pesto Sauce

[MAKES 4 SERVINGS]

Grilled lobster is the epitome of summertime dining pleasure. Split lobsters are brushed with an intense citrus-herb pesto as they grill. The shells turn brick red, the meat becomes creamy white and charred by the grill, and the flavor is superb. It's all very simple and so much what modern Italian cooking is all about: excellent ingredients prepared in a simple manner to complement the food's natural tastes and textures. Serve with a large tossed green salad, perhaps one with shaved fennel and radishes.

When buying lobsters, look for those that are frisky. When they are picked up out of the water, the tail should curl tightly under the body. When cooked, the meat is more tender.

Four 1½- to 1¾-pound lobsters

8 tablespoons (1 stick) unsalted butter, softened

Grated zest of 1 lime

Grated zest of 1 orange

Grated zest of 1 lemon

1 clove garlic, minced

1 tablespoon minced fresh rosemary leaves

¼ cup finely chopped flat-leaf parsley

Sea salt and freshly ground black pepper

To kill the lobster quickly, plunge a very sharp knife into the natural cross located at the back of the lobster's head between the eyes. Then pull the knife sharply down the body to split it in half. Turn and cut the other side in half. If desired, remove the sac from the head and the veins running the length of the body.

Heat a charcoal or gas grill until hot. If using a barbecue, position the coals about 4 inches from the heat. Heat the coals until they are white hot.

In a small bowl, combine the butter and lime, orange, and lemon zests. Add the garlic,

rosemary, and parsley and stir until smooth. Season to taste with salt and pepper. Divide the pesto into two bowls and set one aside to use just before serving. Using a pastry brush, lightly paint the fleshy side of the lobster with half of the citrus pesto. Place the lobsters, flesh side down, on the grates and cook until the shell turns bright red, 3 to 5 minutes.

Turn, brush the meat again with the pesto, and cook until the meat is opaque, 4 to 6 minutes more. (Alternatively, broil them under a preheated broiler, with the pan about 4 inches from the heat, for 3 to 5 minutes, then turn and cook until the meat is opaque, 4 to 6 minutes more.) To serve, place the halved lobsters on 4 large plates and spoon the reserved pesto on top.

Salmone in Padella con Prugne, Pesche e Pomodori
Pan-Roasted Salmon with Black Plums, Peaches, and Tomatoes

[MAKES 4 SERVINGS]

When summer stone fruits are at the height of their season, and the air is perfumed with their scent, that's the time to serve this mildly spicy, tangy-sweet sauce to complement rich salmon. Sautéed Farmer-Style Spinach (page 188) would be a beautiful and tasty accompaniment for the fish.

½ pound ripe tomatoes

¾ pound ripe peaches

¾ pound black plums

1 tablespoon unsalted butter

1 tablespoon finely chopped garlic

2 medium shallots, finely chopped (3 tablespoons)

¼ cup lightly packed fresh basil leaves

Pinch of red pepper flakes

¼ cup sugar

½ cup cider vinegar

Sea salt and freshly ground black pepper

Four 6- to 7-ounce salmon fillets, patted dry with paper towels

2 tablespoons extra-virgin olive oil

Core the tomatoes and cut a small "x" in each base. Fill a pot three-quarters full of water and bring to a boil. Add the tomatoes and cook until the skin begins to peel away from the base, about 1 minute. Remove with a slotted spoon and set aside until they are cool enough to handle. Using a sharp paring knife, peel off the skin. (If it doesn't come off easily, return the tomatoes to boiling water for 10 to 20 seconds longer, depending on how ripe they are.)

Slice the tomatoes in half crosswise. Holding each half in the palm of your hand, gently squeeze out the seeds and discard. Cut the tomatoes into ¾-inch dice and set aside.

Return the water to a boil, add the peaches and plums, and cook for 30 seconds. Remove with a slotted spoon and set aside until cool enough to handle. Using a sharp paring knife, peel off the skin. Cut the fruits in half and remove the stones. Cut into ¾-inch dice and set aside.

In a large heavy skillet, melt the butter over medium-high heat. Add the garlic, shallots, basil, and pepper flakes, partially cover, and cook for 1 to 2 minutes. Uncover, stir in the peaches, plums, and tomatoes, and cook, stirring occasionally, until they start to soften, 2 to 3 minutes. Add the sugar and cook, stirring, until melted. Add the vinegar and cook over low heat, stirring occasionally, until the fruits are completely soft, 5 to 6 minutes longer. Transfer the mixture to a food processor and pulse until it is chunky-smooth. Season to taste with salt and pepper. Pour into a bowl and set aside.

Lightly brush the salmon with olive oil. Season with salt and pepper. Heat the remaining oil in a large skillet over medium-high heat. Add the salmon and pan-roast it until lightly browned, 3 to 4 minutes. Turn and cook the second side for 3 to 4 minutes more for medium-rare. (Cook the second side for about 5 minutes for medium.) Remove and serve each fillet with a generous spoonful of fruit salsa drizzled across the fish. Pass the remaining salsa at the table.

Dentice al Rosmarino con Cicoria e Fagioli
Roasted Red Snapper with Chicory and White Beans

[MAKES 4 SERVINGS]

Red snapper is a sturdy, sweet-tasting fish that stands up well to partners like the hearty country-style chicory and beans that I serve with it here. Try to buy one large fish—about 3½ pounds—for this dish because whole fish cooked on the bone is more moist and flavorful. Also, the pieces are less likely to fall apart when you fillet and serve it. If no large fish are available, substitute four 1½-pound red snappers.

I also suggest serving this with *Salmoriglio* Sauce (page 109) or simply olive oil with a little lemon juice added to it. During the final cooking, the beans and tomato partially break down, adding a saucelike creaminess to the combination. Chicory is delicious with delicately flavored striped bass, but you could use mustard greens or chard, if you prefer.

½ cup dried cannellini beans, or substitute
    1 cup rinsed and drained canned white beans

1 large bulb fennel

4 tablespoons extra-virgin olive oil, plus extra for drizzling

One 3½-pound red snapper, cleaned, scaled, and gutted,
    or four 1½-pound red snappers

Rosemary Salt (page 253) or sea salt with a pinch of dried
    or minced fresh rosemary leaves added

Freshly ground black pepper

1 large yellow onion, sliced (1½ cups)

8 lemon slices, plus 1 lemon cut in half for squeezing

8 sprigs fresh rosemary

2 tablespoons finely chopped pancetta

continued

2 cloves garlic, crushed

2 pounds chicory, trimmed, washed, dried, cut into 1-inch pieces
(about 8 cups)

Pinch of red pepper flakes

1 cup grape tomatoes, cut in half

Salmoriglio Sauce (optional; page 109), for serving

About 2 hours before cooking the fish, add the beans to a pot and cover with cold water. Bring the water to a boil for 2 minutes, then remove from the heat, cover the pan, and let stand for 1 hour. Drain the beans and cover with at least twice as much cold water. Bring to a gentle boil and cook until just tender, about 1 hour, then drain again. Set aside. (This can be done a day ahead of time.)

Preheat the oven to 450°F.

Trim the fronds and stalks from the fennel and cut it in half lengthwise. Core the bulb, then cut it crosswise into ¼-inch slices.

Line a sheet pan with aluminum foil. Drizzle a little olive oil over both sides of the fish and lay it on the tray. Season the fish with Rosemary Salt and pepper. Fill the cavity with the onion, fennel, lemon slices, and rosemary sprigs. Wrap butcher twine around the fish, tying it closed at four or five places. Bake the fish in the oven until the meat is just opaque at the bone when pricked with a fork and the gills start to lift up, 30 to 35 minutes. If using small fish, this will take about 20 to 25 minutes. (An instant-read thermometer inserted in the thickest point should register 145°F for proper doneness.)

While the fish is cooking, heat the 4 tablespoons of olive oil in a large skillet over medium-high heat until hot. Add the pancetta and cook, stirring, until lightly colored, about 1 minute. Add the garlic, cook for 30 seconds, then stir in the chicory, pepper flakes, and salt and pepper to taste. Cook, stirring constantly, for 2 minutes. Cover the skillet, turn the heat down to medium-low, and cook until the chicory is tender, 2 to 4 minutes. Stir in the white beans and tomatoes and cook until heated through and the tomatoes begin to break down, 4 to 5 minutes. Taste to adjust the seasonings and keep warm.

When the fish is cooked, remove it from the oven and place it to one side of a large serving platter. Using a medium-size knife, cut across the body below the gills and discard the head. Make another cut just above the tail and remove it.

Using a knife or the back of a spoon, start at the bottom of the fish and make an incision into one side of the fish above the skeleton and cut around the body, gently lifting up the flesh slightly as you do this. Continue cutting along the second side of the fish.

Using a wide spatula, gently work it along the rib cage to loosen the meat from the bones. Do the same for the other side. Flip the fillet, skin side down, to the other side of the plate. Lift off the skeleton in one piece and discard. Remove any pin bones that remain on the fillets.

Transfer the fillets to a platter and season with Rosemary Salt and pepper. Squeeze fresh lemon juice on top and drizzle with a little olive oil. Cut the fish into 4 generous portions and serve the fillets, skin side up, on 4 large plates with a generous spoonful of the chicory and white beans. Serve accompanied with Salmoriglio Sauce, if desired and set aside.

Zuppa di Pesce
Fish Soup

[MAKES 4 SERVINGS]

This is a grand dish to serve for a special occasion, such as *la Vigilia de Natale,* or Christmas Eve. While it will take some planning and, perhaps, ordering the different shellfish ahead of time, I think you will be pleased by the results. It is one of my favorite soups with shellfish and white fish. In the kitchen, we often say, "Here comes flavor!" when talking about its vibrant tastes and colors.

You will notice that I use both raw and canned tomatoes in this soup because each adds a different flavor and texture. Also, olive oil imparts different tastes depending on when it is used during the cooking. In this dish, it is both a medium in which to sauté the onion and garlic, as well as a final flavor enhancer that is drizzled on before serving.

5 tablespoons extra-virgin olive oil, plus extra for drizzling

1 small yellow onion, chopped (½ cup)

4 cloves garlic, crushed, plus garlic halves for rubbing bread

1 pint grape or cherry tomatoes, cut in half

One 14.5-ounce can chopped tomatoes

2 cups dry white wine, such as Pinot Grigio or Trebbiano

2 sprigs fresh basil

½ teaspoon red pepper flakes

Four 5-ounce white fish fillets, such as sea bass, halibut, or swordfish

4 thick-cut slices Italian bread, about 6 inches in diameter, grilled or lightly toasted

6 large shrimp, with heads on, if possible, peeled and deveined

½ pound mussels, scrubbed and debearded

½ pound Manila, cherrystone, or littleneck clams, scrubbed and purged (see page 122)

½ pound squid bodies, cleaned and sliced into ½-inch rings

Sea salt and freshly ground black pepper

¼ cup chopped flat-leaf parsley

In a large, deep nonreactive pot, heat the olive oil over medium-high heat. Add the onion and garlic and cook, stirring, until transparent, about 5 minutes. Add the fresh and chopped tomatoes and cook, stirring occasionally, for 2 minutes. Stir in the wine, basil, and pepper flakes, bring the liquid to a boil, and cook for 2 to 3 minutes.

Add the fish fillets, adjust the heat down so the liquid is simmering, and cook for 5 to 6 minutes. Meanwhile, grill or toast the bread slices, then rub them with garlic, and set aside.

Add the shrimp, mussels, clams, and squid to the pot, cover, and cook until the mussels and clams have opened and the shrimp and squid are cooked, 2 to 3 minutes. Season to taste with salt and pepper. Discard any shellfish that do not open.

Using a spatula, carefully remove the fish and shellfish to 4 wide soup bowls. Sprinkle chopped parsley over the fish, drizzle with olive oil, and serve with grilled bread.

pollame e carni

Pollo Arrosto Roast Chicken *Pollo Marinato in Aceto Balsamico* Chicken Marinated in Balsamic Vinegar *Piccione con Rapini, Zucca e Porcini* Roast Squab with Broccoli Rabe, Butternut Squash, and Porcini Mushrooms *Fagiano al Mattone* Brick-Roasted Pheasant *Coniglio con Polenta e Olive* Rabbit with Polenta and Sicilian Olives *Tonno di Coniglio* Rabbit Braised in Oil Piedmont Style *Arrosto di Maiale con Pesche* Roasted Pork with Glazed Peaches *Involtini di Maiale* Herbed Pork Rolls *Animelle con Piselli al Marsala* Veal Sweetbreads with Peas and Marsala *Nodino di Vitello, Cipolline in Agrodolce e Asparagi* Seared Veal Chop with Sweet and Sour Cipollini Onions and Roasted Asparagus *Ragù di Agnello con Rigatoni* Hearty Lamb Ragout with Rigatoni *Arrosto di Agnello con Pancetta* Roast Leg of Lamb Wrapped in Pancetta *Tagliata di Manzo* Sliced Steak with Rosemary *Carré di Agnello con Rapini e Patate con Salsa al Vino Rosso* Rack of Lamb with Broccoli Rabe and Potatoes and Red Wine Sauce *Brasato di Manzo* Braised Short Ribs *Bollito Misto* Assorted Boiled Meats *Stufato di Capriolo alla Süd Tirolese* South Tyrolean Venison Stew

POULTRY and MEAT

Americans are fortunate to have some of the richest, most tender grass- or grain-fed beef in the world. While few regions in Italy have such fine beef, the meat from the large, white Chianina cows, raised in the lush, grassy fields around Arezzo, in Tuscany, is exceptional. Bistecca alla Fiorentina, served in nearby Florence, is one of their most famous dishes.

Like much of the meat and poultry in Italy, these large porterhouse steaks are either grilled over an open hearth or pan-roasted on top of the stove. This is because in earlier times, few kitchens had an oven, so direct heat was the only cooking option. High heat sears the outside and adds a rich color; it also seals in the juices. The results are extraordinary steaks. Although large porterhouse steaks are a rarity in the rest of Italy, locals and visitors to Florence can't seem to get enough of them.

In this chapter, you will notice that I also pan-sear many dishes. Judging by the popularity of my Sliced Steak with Rosemary done in this style (page 167), Americans approve. Sage-scented veal chop with sweet and sour onions is similarly cooked in a skillet (page 160). It is perhaps our most popular main course at Fiamma. Once seared, the chop is finished in the oven. I do this with any cut of meat or a bird that is too thick or dense to cook through on the stovetop without the outside becoming overly charred.

Another roasted dish—pork loin served with peaches glazed with chestnut honey (page 154)—is a showstopper. The tangy sweet fruit slices elegantly accent the chops. Like most main courses in Italy, however, it is relatively simple. Perhaps that is because, in the grand scheme of Italian dining, antipasti and pasta have already taken the edge off appetites.

Whether a dish is simple or substantial, Italians like flavor, and they have a great fondness for succulent stews and braised meats in heady sauces. Any cut of meat, including veal, lamb, pork, or game, that comes from the less tender, working parts of the animal (not the ribs or loins) is generally slowly cooked on top of the stove in an aromatic liquid until tender.

Even the most sophisticated and "modern" Americans have a similar fondness for such comfort foods. In the last few years, short ribs have become a fixture on menus across the country. Along with our fall-off-the-bone tender Braised Short Ribs (page 172), other hearty and satisfying dishes to tempt you in this chapter include venison stew from Italy's Alto Adige region near the Austrian border and the intensely flavorful, olive oil-simmered Rabbit in "Tonno" (page 151).

Cooking foods in *tonno* is similar to making duck confit in which the birds are slowly braised in their own fat. The early Piemontese learned to preserve foods with this technique from neighboring Ligurians who used it to store fresh-caught tuna for long periods of time.

In my travels throughout Italy, I noted that the terrain became harsher to the east and south of Rome. Abruzzo and Puglia, once an ancient Greek colony, are provinces characterized by sharp mountainous cliffs. The hills are dotted with countless sheep. As a result, lamb is the meat of choice and the dairy products, including Pecorino Romano, are made with ewe's milk. Since I married a woman from Molise, in this region, I have come to appreciate lamb in many guises, including the *Ragù* of Lamb (page 163), Roast Leg of Lamb Wrapped in Pancetta (page 165), and Rack of Lamb (page 169) in this chapter.

If the United States has the advantage with its beef, I think most of our poultry doesn't come close to Italian birds. That is especially true when I compare American chickens with the wonderful white Leghorn chickens, with the long breast and short legs, originally from the city of Livorno.

However, I will quickly add that some excellent free-range chickens and game birds are becoming more readily available to Americans, even in supermarkets. The quality of the bird can make a marked difference in how a dish tastes. At the end of the book, I have listed some sources for poultry and game birds. One advantage of buying game birds here is that they come cleaned and dressed. In Italy you always have to clean them.

You will certainly appreciate the flavor in simple Italian-style roasted chicken where there is absolutely nothing besides a few aromatic vegetables and Rosemary Salt (a staple I find indispensable) to camouflage the bird's natural taste. Similarly, there is little to disguise the real taste of a pheasant pan-roasted with a brick, or *mattone,* on top. It is deliciously crispy on the outside and juicy inside (page 147).

Cut-up birds cooked in the oven, or fricasseed, are also popular in Italy. In this chapter, a capon or large chicken is roasted with balsamic vinegar, mustard, herbs, wine, and stock (page 142). It is as savory a chicken in a pot as you will ever taste.

Finally, a word about innards. In the days when meat was very precious, and small amounts were used more as a flavoring than the principle ingredient in a dish, nothing was ever thrown away. There are many old Italian recipes for sweetbreads, kidneys, etc. One of my favorite versions is sweetbreads prepared the way I first tasted them in Rome. The cleaned and blanched sweetbreads are sliced, lightly dusted with flour, and sautéed, then served with peas and Marsala sauce.

This chapter is a bit of a tour of Italy—Rome, Abruzzo, Tuscany, Piemonte, and the Alto Adige. That is contemporary Italian: using provisions from the entire peninsula.

Pollo Arrosto
Roast Chicken

[MAKES 4 SERVINGS]

There is nothing better than walking into my house and smelling the wonderful aroma of garlic- and herb-scented roast chicken coming from the kitchen. Along with the juicy meat, scraping up those caramelized bits of vegetables and garlic from the bottom of the roasting pan—the *sugo de arrosto*—with chunks of country bread is one of life's greatest simple pleasures.

Roast chicken is a staple throughout Italy and each region has its own style of seasoning. In Emilia-Romagna, for example, rosemary and sage or thyme are characteristic. Use any side dish in this book to accompany it. This chicken is also delicious when served at room temperature with *Salmoriglio* Sauce (page 109) or Wild Mushroom Mayonnaise, *Maionese di Funghi* (page 262).

One 3½- to 3¾-pound whole chicken, excess fat removed, rinsed under cold water and patted dry with paper towels

Rosemary Salt (page 253), or sea salt with a pinch of dried or minced fresh rosemary leaves added, and freshly ground black pepper

¼ cup fresh rosemary leaves

¼ cup fresh thyme leaves

2 heads garlic, loose papery outer skin removed, cut in half horizontally

3 medium yellow onions, chopped

3 carrots, peeled and cut into thick slices

2 ribs celery, trimmed and chopped

1 lemon, cut in half

¼ cup extra-virgin olive oil

Preheat the oven to 375°F.

Season the chicken inside and out with Rosemary Salt and pepper. Put half of the rosemary and thyme and both heads of garlic inside the bird's cavity along with half of the onions, carrots, and celery, and the lemon. Tie the legs together, tuck the wingtips under the wings, and drizzle the olive oil over the chicken.

Scatter the remaining onions, carrots, and celery in the bottom of a heavy roasting pan just large enough to hold the chicken and lay the chicken on top of them. Transfer the pan to the oven and roast, basting with the pan juices every 20 minutes, for 1¾ to 2 hours, or until an instant-read thermometer measures 165°F when stuck deep into the leg socket and the chicken's juices run clear. Remove the chicken from the oven and let it rest for 30 minutes before carving and serving.

Pollo Marinato in Aceto Balsamico
Chicken Marinated in Balsamic Vinegar

[MAKES 4 TO 6 SERVINGS]

H ere's my idea of a perfect summer night's meal: this mouth-watering, juicy oven-roasted chicken served hot or at room temperature with Insalata di Misticanza (page 5). Actually, it's pretty terrific no matter what the weather or season.

½ cup balsamic vinegar

⅓ cup freshly squeezed lemon juice

2 tablespoons Dijon mustard

2 tablespoons olive oil

1 teaspoon red pepper flakes

2 cloves garlic, minced

Leaves from 2 sprigs fresh rosemary

2 sprigs fresh thyme

One 4-pound capon or chicken, with excess fat removed,
    cut into 8 pieces

Sea salt and freshly ground black pepper

½ cup Homemade Chicken Stock (page 255) or canned low-sodium stock

1 teaspoon grated lemon zest

1 tablespoon chopped fresh flat-leaf parsley

At least a few hours before you plan to serve the chicken, in a small bowl, whisk together the vinegar, lemon juice, mustard, olive oil, pepper flakes, and garlic. Combine the vinaigrette, rosemary, thyme sprigs, and chicken pieces in a large resealable plastic bag. Seal the bag, toss to coat the chicken, and refrigerate for 3 hours or overnight, turning the bag occasionally.

Preheat the oven to 425°F.

Remove the chicken from the bag and pat the pieces dry with paper towels. Season the pieces with salt and pepper and arrange them, skin side up, in a heavy baking dish just large enough to hold the pieces in a single layer. Roast until the chicken is just cooked through, about 1 hour. Transfer the chicken to a serving platter.

On top of the stove, place the baking dish over medium-high heat. Stir the chicken stock into the pan drippings, scraping up any browned bits on the bottom of the pan with a wooden spoon, and bring to a boil. Spoon the sauce over the chicken, sprinkle on the lemon zest and parsley, and serve.

Piccione con Rapini, Zucca e Porcini
Roast Squab with Broccoli Rabe, Butternut Squash, and Porcini Mushrooms

[MAKES 4 SERVINGS]

Squabs are small, all dark-meat birds. For this luxurious main course, they are roasted until richly browned and succulent, then served on a colorful bed of mixed vegetables. I fell in love with squabs in Italy, but American birds from California, New York, and Vermont are quite wonderful, especially because they are cleaned, plucked, and dressed when you buy them, making it much easier to prepare them.

½ medium yellow onion, chopped (½ cup)

1 medium carrot, peeled and chopped (¼ cup)

1 medium rib celery, trimmed and chopped (¼ cup)

1 head garlic, broken into cloves but with the skins left on

2 sprigs fresh rosemary

1 sprig fresh sage

Four 1-pound squabs, first two wing joints and excess skin removed and discarded, rinsed under cold water and patted dry with paper towels

Sea salt and freshly ground black pepper

4 to 5 tablespoons extra-virgin olive oil

1 cup dry white wine, such as Pinot Grigio or Trebbiano

2 cups Rich Chicken Stock (page 256)

1 bunch broccoli rabe, coarse stems discarded and chopped into 3-inch pieces

¼ pound pancetta, cut into small cubes

continued

1 cup peeled and cubed (¼-inch pieces) butternut squash

1 pound fresh porcini or cremini mushrooms, wiped, trimmed,
and thickly sliced

2 tablespoons chopped flat-leaf parsley, for garnish

Preheat the oven to 400°F.

Scatter the onion, carrot, celery, garlic cloves, rosemary, and sage in the bottom of a roasting pan just large enough to hold the squabs comfortably in a single layer. Season the birds with salt and pepper and drizzle with 2 tablespoons of the olive oil. Lay the squabs, breast side up, on the vegetables and put the pan in the oven to roast until the birds are richly browned and the legs move easily in the socket, about 25 minutes, basting twice during this time.

Remove the pan from the oven, transfer the birds to a warm platter, lightly tent with aluminum foil, and set aside to rest. On top of the stove, pour the white wine into the roasting pan and bring to a boil over high heat, scraping up any browned bits. Cook until the wine has almost evaporated, then pour in the chicken stock and simmer over medium heat for 10 minutes.

Strain the liquid into a clean saucepan, pressing the vegetables with a wooden spoon to extract as much liquid as possible. Discard the vegetables. Skim the fat from the surface of the sauce and, if necessary, cook over high heat until reduced by half, or until the sauce is thick enough to lightly coat the back of a wooden spoon, 8 to 10 minutes. Taste to adjust the seasonings, and set aside over low heat.

While the sauce reduces, bring a large pot of salted water to a boil. Add the broccoli rabe and cook until it is bright green and just tender, 3 to 4 minutes, then drain, shock under cold water, and drain again. Set aside.

In a large deep skillet, cook the pancetta in 2 tablespoons of the olive oil over medium heat, stirring occasionally, until lightly browned, 3 to 4 minutes. Add the butternut squash and cook, stirring, until it is lightly colored on all sides, 4 to 5 minutes. Stir in the reserved broccoli rabe and the mushrooms, and continue cooking, stirring occasionally, until the vegetables are well blended and tender, 4 to 5 minutes more. Season with salt, pepper, and additional olive oil to taste.

Mound the vegetables on a large serving platter and lay the squabs on top. Spoon the sauce over the birds, sprinkle on a little parsley, and serve immediately.

Fagiano al Mattone
Brick-Roasted Pheasant

[MAKES 4 SERVINGS]

One bite of this crispy, juicy pheasant will fill your mouth with the luscious tastes of herbs and juicy meat. The split birds are cooked in a cast-iron skillet with a foil-wrapped brick (*mattone*) placed on top to keep it flat and ensure even cooking (see Note). It is similar to *Pollo alla Diavola,* the well-known Tuscan chicken dish with spicy red pepper in lemon marinade. Serve the pheasant hot or at room temperature with Rosemary Roasted Potatoes on page 193 and sautéed escarole.

When cooking birds in a hot pan, dry the skin very well so they won't stick or tear when turning them.

2 whole pheasants, 2¾ to 3 pounds each, rinsed under cold water and patted dry with paper towels

Juice of 4 lemons

4 sprigs fresh rosemary

3 to 4 sprigs fresh thyme

4 large peeled cloves garlic

Sea salt

½ cup extra-virgin olive oil

Freshly ground black pepper

2 bricks, wrapped in heavy-duty aluminum foil

At least 5 hours before you plan to serve the pheasants, with a sharp knife, cut off the first two wing joints from the pheasants and discard. Remove the backbone by cutting along either side of it with kitchen shears. Open each bird like a book and turn it flesh side down with the legs closest to you. Starting at the bottom point of the breastbone, and using your thumb and index finger, pull up on the cartilage and bone, working it loose from the breasts. If desired, remove the rib bones by carefully working a sharp knife between the ribs and the flesh, starting at the bottom of the breast, and working up toward the wing. Flip the rib cage back and chop off the bones. Or have the butcher do this. Put the pheasants in a large, flat, nonreactive pan or bowl. Pour on the lemon juice.

Remove the leaves from the rosemary and thyme sprigs and finely chop them with the garlic and 2 tablespoons salt. Add the olive oil and mix well. Pour half of the mixture over the inside of the pheasants, rubbing it into the meat. Turn the pheasants skin side up and spread the remaining herb mixture over and under the skin, then season the birds with pepper. Cover and refrigerate in the marinade, skin side up, for at least 4 hours or overnight.

Remove the pheasants from the refrigerator about 1 hour before cooking them to return to room temperature. Dry well with paper towels.

Meanwhile, preheat the oven to 375°F.

Heat one very large or two medium size, well-seasoned, heavy cast-iron skillets over high heat until very hot. Lightly brush them with olive oil, then lay the pheasants, skin side down, in the pans. Immediately place the foil-covered bricks over the birds, pressing down to flatten them. Let the pheasants cook undisturbed until the skin is browned and crisp, about 12 minutes, then remove bricks, turn the birds over, replace the bricks, and cook the second side for 10 minutes.

Transfer the pan to the oven and continue cooking until the juices run clear when pricked in the deepest part of the thigh, 8 to 10 minutes. Remove the pheasants from the oven and transfer them to a warm platter and tent with aluminum foil. Let them stand for 15 minutes before cutting them into leg and breast portions, then serve.

Note: An oven-safe dish with a pound of weight placed in it can be substituted for the bricks. But the weight should not completely cover the skillet or the bird will steam. Some cookware stores sells circular clay disks that fit inside cast-iron skillets expressly for this purpose.

Cooking Juicy Pheasants

People complain that pheasants are sometimes tough or dry. Simple ways to avoid this are to bard the breast with pancetta or butter before cooking or to put some fat between the breast meat and skin. Cook the birds slowly in moist heat or quickly pan-roast them over high heat. Above all, don't overcook pheasants. The meat should be pale pink when served. Another suggestion to keep the bird from drying out is to roast a whole pheasant with the breast down or on its side, so the juices run toward the breast.

Coniglio con Polenta e Olive
Rabbit with Polenta and Sicilian Olives

Fragrant braised rabbit and creamy polenta are a soul-satisfying combination that will leave you feeling content and well nourished. The green Sicilian olives used here are larger than most varieties. They have an assertive, herbaceous taste that adds a perfect top note of flavor to the sauce.

One 2- to 2½-pound rabbit, rinsed under cold water, patted dry
    with paper towels, and cut into serving pieces

Sea salt and freshly ground black pepper

6 tablespoons extra-virgin olive oil

1 medium-large onion, diced (1 cup)

1 large carrot, peeled and diced (½ cup)

1 large rib celery, trimmed and diced (½ cup)

3 large cloves garlic, chopped

3 sprigs fresh thyme

2 sprigs fresh rosemary

1 cup dry white wine, such as Trebbiano or Pinot Grigio

2 cups Homemade Chicken Stock (page 255) or canned low-sodium stock

One 28-ounce can Italian tomatoes, undrained

1¼ cups sliced brine-cured Sicilian green olives
    (about 7 ounces whole olives with pits)

1 cup coarse yellow cornmeal or instant polenta

2 tablespoons unsalted butter

¼ cup freshly grated Parmigiano-Reggiano cheese (about 1 ounce)

Flat-leaf parsley sprigs, for garnish

Preheat the oven to 375°F.

Season the rabbit liberally with salt and pepper. Heat 4 tablespoons of the olive oil in a large, heavy pot or Dutch oven over medium-high heat. Working in two batches, add the rabbit to the pot and brown on all sides, turning often, 6 to 8 minutes per batch. Keep the oil hot so that with each addition it sizzles, and do not crowd the pieces or the meat will steam and not brown. Transfer the browned rabbit pieces to a bowl.

Reduce the heat to medium and add the remaining 2 tablespoons of olive oil to the pot. Stir in the onion, carrot, and celery and cook, stirring often and scraping up the browned bits from the bottom of the pan, until the onion is translucent and the vegetables are beginning to soften, about 5 minutes. Add the garlic, thyme, and rosemary and cook, stirring, for 2 minutes more. Pour in the wine, cook for 1 minute, then stir in the stock. Add the tomatoes to the pot, crushing them with your hands as you add them, then stir in the olives. Bring the liquid to a simmer and cook for 4 to 5 minutes, then return the rabbit to the pot. Cover the pot and transfer it to the oven for 45 minutes to 1 hour, or until the rabbit is fork tender.

Meanwhile, put 3 cups of water and a teaspoon of salt in a large saucepan and bring to a boil. Slowly whisk in the cornmeal in a thin stream until all the polenta is incorporated and the mixture begins to thicken. Switch to a wooden spoon and simmer, stirring constantly, for 30 minutes longer, or until the polenta is cooked. Stir in the butter and cheese and season to taste with salt and pepper. (For instant polenta, cook according to the package instructions.)

Remove the rabbit from the oven, transfer the pieces with a slotted spoon to a warm dish, and tent with aluminum foil. Reduce the sauce over medium-high heat until thickened, 10 to 15 minutes. Spoon the polenta in the centers of 4 large dinner plates or a serving platter. Serve the rabbit on top of the polenta. Spoon the sauce over it, garnish with parsley sprigs, and serve.

Tonno di Coniglio
Rabbit Braised in Oil Piedmont Style

[MAKES 4 SERVINGS]

Early Ligurians who traded with the Piemontese to the north of them taught their neighbors to preserve foods by covering them with oil and slowly cooking them with aromatic herbs and vegetables. Ligurian fishermen typically saved tuna, or *tonno*, this way. After an hour and a half, this rabbit becomes tender and infused with the savory flavors of herbs, vegetables, and earthy porcini mushrooms. If available, I prefer to use the rabbit hind quarters because they are the meatiest section.

4 young rabbit hind leg quarters or 1 young rabbit,
    cut into 6 to 8 serving pieces (see Sources, page 266)

Sea salt and freshly ground black pepper

½ pound fresh porcini or cremini mushrooms, wiped, stems trimmed,
    and quartered

1 medium yellow onion, cut into ¼-inch dice (¾ cup)

1 medium carrot, peeled and cut into ¼-inch dice (⅓ cup)

1 medium rib celery, trimmed and diced (⅓ cup)

2 shallots, chopped

1 head garlic, loose papery outer skin removed and sliced in half horizontally

3 large sprigs fresh rosemary

3 large sprigs fresh sage

½ tablespoon whole juniper berries

½ tablespoon whole black peppercorns

2 to 3 cups olive oil, for covering the rabbit

4 cups mixed salad greens, washed and dried

Juice of 1 lemon

151

Preheat the oven to 350°F. Season the rabbit liberally with salt and pepper. Put the rabbit, mushrooms, onion, carrot, celery, shallots, garlic, rosemary, sage, juniper berries, and peppercorns in a heavy pot just large enough to hold the rabbit in a single layer. Pour on enough olive oil to cover. Transfer to the oven and cook until the rabbit is fork tender, 1 to 1½ hours. Begin testing after 1 hour. Remove the pot from the oven and let the rabbit cool to room temperature in the pot.

Toss the mixed greens in a bowl with 3 to 4 tablespoons of the olive oil from the pot used to cook the rabbit. Add the lemon juice and salt and pepper to taste, and toss. Divide the salad among 4 large plates.

Cut the meat from the bones and place the pieces of rabbit on top of the mixed greens. Spoon the mushrooms and vegetables over the rabbit and serve immediately.

Save That Fragrant Oil

Once you serve this dish, the fragrant oil and pan juices that are left can be separated and used again in other dishes. Skim off the oil from the top of the pot with a large spoon and strain it. Or pour all of the contents into a separator and divide the oil from the juices. Diced potatoes fried in the oil are superb. The pan juices can be used to enrich hearty soups.

Arrosto di Maiale con Pesche
Roasted Pork with Glazed Peaches

[MAKES 4 SERVINGS]

When summer arrives in the small
hill town of Castel del Rio, in Emilia-Romagna, stands along the road are piled high with gorgeous
ripe peaches. People devour the juicy, warm white or yellow peach right there, out of hand,
so each stand also has a little spigot for rinsing afterward. This town is also known for
their chestnuts that are celebrated during an annual festival.
Peaches glazed with sweet and subtly bitter chestnut honey reduced with
white wine vinegar and a sprig of rosemary are the enticing addition to pork roast.
I salivate just thinking about them.

1 center-cut bone-in pork rib roast, about 5 pounds, well trimmed and
  chine bone removed (3½ to 4 pounds trimmed weight)

Extra-virgin olive oil

Rosemary Salt (page 253), or sea salt with a pinch of dried or
  minced fresh rosemary leaves added, and freshly ground black pepper

6 small sprigs fresh rosemary

1 large yellow onion, coarsely chopped (1¼ cups)

2 small carrots, peeled and coarsely chopped (¾ cup)

2 small ribs celery, trimmed and coarsely chopped (¾ cup)

1 head garlic, loose papery outer skin removed, and cut in half horizontally

Chestnut Honey Glazed Peaches (recipe follows)

4 cups dry white wine, such as Pinot Grigio or Trebbiano

2 cups Homemade Chicken Stock (page 255) or canned low-sodium stock

Coarse sea salt

Preheat the oven to 375°F.

Brush the pork with olive oil and season it liberally with Rosemary Salt and black pepper. Lay the rosemary sprigs on top of the roast and secure them in several places with butcher's twine.

Sprinkle 2 tablespoons of olive oil into a large heavy skillet or roasting pan and set it over high heat until almost smoking. Place the roast, fat side down, in the pan and sear it on all sides including the ends until richly browned, about 10 minutes total cooking time. Add another tablespoon of oil to the pan along with the onion, carrots, celery, and garlic and cook, stirring occasionally, for 3 to 4 minutes.

Pour in 2 cups of the wine. Transfer the pan to the oven and cook until a meat thermometer inserted in the thickest part of the roast registers 150°F, 50 minutes to 1 hour. If the tops of the bones begin to burn, cover them with aluminum foil. Transfer the roast to a cutting board. Tent it lightly with foil and let it rest for 20 to 25 minutes for the juices to be reabsorbed.

Meanwhile, prepare the Chestnut Honey Glazed Peaches.

On top of the stove, set the pan with the vegetables over medium heat. Pour in the remaining 2 cups of white wine, scraping up the brown bits on the bottom of the pan. Add the chicken stock, raise the heat to high, and boil until the liquid is reduced by half. Season to taste with Rosemary Salt.

Pour the liquid through a fine strainer, pressing on the vegetables to extract as much liquid as possible. Discard the vegetables. Skim off as much fat as possible and reserve the liquid.

Remove the string and carve the roast between the chops. Serve the meat on a platter drizzled with some of the sauce. Add the peaches. Spoon a little sauce over them, and sprinkle on sea salt. Serve family style and pass the extra sauce at the table.

Chestnut Honey Glazed Peaches

2 tablespoons butter

6 firm, ripe, unpeeled peaches, pitted and cut into eighths

⅓ cup chestnut or other honey

⅓ cup white wine vinegar

1 sprig fresh rosemary

Heat the butter in a large skillet over high heat until melted and sizzling. Add the peaches and cook, shaking the pan often, until lightly browned on both sides, 3 to 4 minutes total. Spoon on the honey, stir to blend, and cook until it has dissolved, 30 seconds to 1 minute. Pour in the vinegar, adjust the heat to medium-high, and cook, stirring occasionally, for 2 to 3 minutes. Add the rosemary sprig and cook until the peaches are well glazed, 4 to 5 minutes more.

Involtini di Maiale
Herbed Pork Rolls

[MAKES 4 SERVINGS]

Classically, *involtini* are thin slices of veal or beef that are stuffed and rolled. In this version, I season sliced pork tenderloin with fresh herbs and Pecorino Romano cheese before rolling them.

One 1½-pound boneless pork tenderloin, cut on the extreme diagonal into 12 slices

Sea salt and freshly ground black pepper

¼ cup freshly grated Pecorino Romano cheese

1½ teaspoons finely chopped fresh sage

1 teaspoon finely chopped fresh rosemary leaves

1 teaspoon minced garlic

¼ cup all-purpose flour

3 tablespoons extra-virgin olive oil

1 cup dry white wine, such as Pinot Grigio or Trebbiano

On a flat work surface, lightly pound the pork slices until they are a scant ¼ inch thick. Season with salt and pepper. In a bowl, combine the Pecorino, sage, rosemary, and garlic. Sprinkle 1 teaspoon of the herb mixture over each pork slice, roll it into a cylinder, and secure each with a toothpick. Season the rolls with salt and pepper.

Put the flour in a flat bowl. Lightly coat the pork rolls with flour, patting to remove the excess.

In a large skillet, heat the oil over medium-high heat until hot. Add the rolls slowly, so each one sizzles as it is added, and cook until browned all over, about 3 minutes, turning with a wooden spatula to cook evenly. Pour in the wine, cover, and simmer until the rolls are cooked through, 3 minutes more. Transfer them to a plate and cover loosely with aluminum foil.

Boil the cooking liquid until it reduces to a thick sauce, about 2 minutes. Return the rolls to the skillet and shake the pan to coat them with sauce. Serve with any remaining sauce spooned over them.

Animelle con Piselli al Marsala
Veal Sweetbreads with Peas and Marsala

Ancient Roman cuisine included several dishes with sweetbreads and other innards because no part of an animal was wasted. They are served here with a fragrant Marsala pan sauce and accented with bright green peas. As an alternative, serve them with *Maionese di Funghi* (page 262) in place of the sauce and drizzle with a little fresh lemon juice and capers. I first tasted sweetbreads, with their slightly crunchy exterior and silky insides, in a small restaurant in Testaccio, an old area of central Rome where the Protestant cemetery is located. Surrounded by stone walls, this tranquil spot, smack in the middle of Rome's insane traffic, is the final resting place of John Keats and Percy Shelley.

2 veal sweetbreads (about 2 pounds each)

1 lemon, cut in quarters

3 tablespoons extra-virgin olive oil

Sea salt and freshly ground black pepper

½ cup all-purpose flour, for dusting

1 medium yellow onion, finely chopped (¾ cup)

2 cloves garlic, crushed

¼ pound thinly sliced prosciutto, cut into ¼-inch strips

¼ cup dry Marsala

1½ cups fresh peas, or substitute defrosted frozen petite peas

½ cup Rich Chicken Stock (page 256)

Finely chopped flat-leaf parsley

At least one day before you plan to serve them, soak the sweetbreads for at least 6 hours (or up to 24 hours) in cold water to remove all traces of blood, changing the water several times, squeezing in some lemon juice with each change. Transfer the sweetbreads to a saucepan filled with cold salted water and bring to a boil. Reduce the heat so the liquid is simmering, cook for 15 minutes, then remove the sweetbreads to a plate until cool enough to handle, 6 to 8 minutes.

Remove and discard all fat, skin, and sinew. Put the sweetbreads in a flat baking pan, cover with a clean towel, and place another baking pan on top of them with a heavy weight on top to flatten them. (A pot filled with water works well.) Refrigerate them for at least 3 hours or up to 24 hours. After pressing, the sweetbreads will be firm; cut them on a slight bias into $1/2$-inch slices.

In a large skillet, heat the olive oil over medium-high heat. Season the sweetbreads with salt and pepper and lightly dust with flour, patting to remove any excess. Add the onion, garlic, and prosciutto to the skillet and cook, stirring, until the onion is translucent, 2 to 3 minutes. Add the sweetbreads and cook, turning once, until golden brown, 3 to 4 minutes per side.

Cover the pan, reduce the heat to medium, and cook until the sweetbreads are tender, 5 to 6 minutes. Once the sweetbreads are cooked, remove them with a slotted spoon to paper towels to drain, then transfer them to a serving platter.

Over high heat, deglaze the pan with the Marsala wine, stirring up all the browned bits, and boil for 2 minutes. Add the peas and chicken stock, and cook over medium-high heat until the peas are tender, 4 to 5 minutes for fresh peas or about 2 minutes for frozen. Season with salt and pepper to taste and spoon the sauce over the sweetbreads. Garnish with parsley and serve.

Nodino di Vitello, Cipolline in Agrodolce e Asparagi
Seared Veal Chop with Sweet and Sour Cipollini Onions and Roasted Asparagus

[MAKES 4 SERVINGS]

This is one of my signature dishes. Juicy veal chops are cooked to perfection—seared on the outside and medium-rare on the inside—and accompanied by sweet and sour *cipollini* (small flat Italian onions) or conventional pearl onions and roasted asparagus. I serve them with Rosemary Roasted Potatoes (page 193), which can cook in the same oven with the veal. The combination is very popular. You will be able to tell when the meat is medium-rare because the chops will puff up a little.

4 tablespoons extra-virgin olive oil

2 tablespoons unsalted butter

1 pound *cipollini* or pearl onions, peeled with an "x" cut in each root end

1½ cups Veal Stock (page 258)

½ cup balsamic vinegar

Four 11- to 12-ounce veal rib chops, about 1¼ inches thick, frenched, trimmed, and patted dry with paper towels

Sea salt and freshly ground black pepper

4 thin slices prosciutto

1 pound large asparagus (about 16 asparagus), peeled and blanched

2 sprigs fresh rosemary

2 sprigs fresh sage

4 large cloves garlic, crushed

½ cup dry white wine, such as Pinot Grigio or Trebbiano

Heat 2 tablespoons of the olive oil and 1 tablespoon of the butter in a large skillet over medium-high heat. Add the *cippolini* or pearl onions and cook, shaking the pan frequently, until lightly browned, about 10 minutes. Pour in ½ cup of the veal stock and the balsamic vinegar and simmer until the onions are tender and most of the liquid has evaporated, 15 to 20 minutes. Keep warm.

While the onions cook, preheat the oven to 400°F.

Season the veal chops liberally with salt and pepper. Heat the remaining 2 tablespoons of the olive oil in a large heavy skillet over medium-high heat until hot. Add the chops and sear on both sides, turning once, 6 to 7 minutes per side. (If they will not fit comfortably in the pan and the oil doesn't sizzle, do this in two pans.) Transfer the pan to the oven and cook until the meat puffs a little for medium-rare, about 10 minutes.

Remove the pan from the oven, transfer the chops to an oven-safe platter, tent with aluminum foil, and let them rest for at least 15 minutes. Leave the oven set at 400°F.

While the chops are in the oven, prepare the asparagus. Lay the prosciutto slices on a piece of parchment or waxed paper. Put 4 asparagus spears on each slice and roll them up. Bake on a sheet pan for 5 to 7 minutes, or until the prosciutto is lightly browned.

Discard the fat in the skillet used to roast the chops. On top of the stove, add the rosemary, sage, garlic, and the remaining tablespoon of butter to the pan. Pour in the wine and bring the liquid to a boil over high heat, stirring up all the browned bits. Cook until the wine evaporates, 4 to 5 minutes. Pour in the remaining cup of veal stock and boil until the sauce is thick enough to coat the back of a wooden spoon, 6 to 8 minutes. Strain the sauce through a fine strainer into a small saucepan and season to taste with salt and pepper.

Before serving, return the veal chops to the oven just long enough to make sure they are hot. Serve each chop on a large dinner plate with some glazed onions spooned over them and a packet of asparagus wrapped in prosciutto alongside it. Drizzle the sauce over the veal and serve.

Ragù di Agnello con Rigatoni
Hearty Lamb Ragout with Rigatoni

[MAKES 4 TO 6 SERVINGS]

In the hills of the Abruzzo or Molise regions
of southern Italy, it is not uncommon to see shepherds walking with flocks of forty or more sheep.
Nowadays, this pastoral image always strikes me as out of character but invariably
it makes me slow down to appreciate the tranquil scenery in these regions.
It follows that the preferred meat for pasta sauce, or ragout, is lamb, unlike in the north
where beef or pork is the choice. Typically the meat is served with spaghetti *alla chitarra,*
a square-cut semolina spaghetti that is now available in America. But rigatoni is a perfect
partner, as well. The thick sauce can be refrigerated for up to
five days or frozen for up to a month.

6 tablespoons extra-virgin olive oil

2 large carrots, peeled and finely chopped (1 cup)

1 large yellow onion, finely chopped (1¼ cups)

1 medium red bell pepper, seeds and membranes removed, finely chopped

4 ounces thickly sliced pancetta, cut into ¼-inch dice

1 pound boneless lamb shoulder, cut into ½-inch dice

¾ cup dry red wine, such as Barbera or Chianti

One 28-ounce can coarsely chopped Italian tomatoes, undrained

1 cup Homemade Chicken Stock (page 255) or canned low-sodium stock

1 bay leaf

½ teaspoon red pepper flakes

Salt and freshly ground black pepper

1 pound dried rigatoni

Freshly grated Pecorino Romano cheese

In a heavy nonreactive, medium-size pot or Dutch oven, heat 4 tablespoons of the olive oil over medium heat until hot. Add the carrots, onion, and bell pepper and cook, stirring occasionally, until softened and just beginning to brown, 8 to 10 minutes. Using a slotted spoon, transfer the vegetables to a plate.

Heat the remaining 2 tablespoons of oil in the pot. Add the pancetta and stir once or twice over medium-high heat until sizzling. Add the lamb and cook, stirring occasionally, until the liquid has evaporated and the meat is browned, about 10 minutes. Do this in batches, if necessary, to keep the oil hot so the meat browns well.

Return the vegetables to the pot. Pour in the red wine and simmer until it has evaporated, scraping up any browned bits in the bottom of the casserole. Add the tomatoes, chicken stock, bay leaf, and pepper flakes. Season to taste with salt and pepper and bring to a boil. Reduce the heat to medium-low, partially cover, and simmer, stirring occasionally, until the lamb is very tender, about 1½ hours. Discard the bay leaf.

Meanwhile, bring a large pot of salted water to a boil. Add the rigatoni and cook until al dente, 12 to 14 minutes, or according to package directions. Drain the rigatoni and toss it with half of the lamb *ragù*. Serve the pasta in large bowls, passing the remaining lamb and the Pecorino cheese at the table.

Square Spaghetti

The *chitarra* is a special tool that resembles a guitar and is used to make this pasta. Fresh pasta dough is pushed with a rolling pin through the wires on the wooden frame of the *chitarra*, thus giving this spaghetti a unique square shape.

Arrosto di Agnello con Pancetta
Roast Leg of Lamb Wrapped in Pancetta

[SERVES 4 TO 6]

My inspiration for this succulent leg
of lamb was the wonderful lamb available in Molise, the region where my wife was born.
Wrapping the meat in thin slices of pancetta helps the potent garlic-herb paste hug the lamb.
Both layers flavor the meat as it roasts and prevents it from drying out.
I prefer lamb roasts cooked to medium because the meat is generally less tough and more flavorful
at that temperature. It is essential to have an instant-read thermometer for cooking meat
because cooking times can vary dramatically, depending on the size and shape of the roast.
The temperature measurement is far more precise.

6 oil-packed anchovy fillets, drained and blotted with paper towels

3 large whole cloves garlic, peeled

2 tablespoons fresh thyme leaves

2 tablespoons fresh rosemary leaves

Finely grated zest of 1 orange

¼ cup extra-virgin olive oil

Salt and freshly ground pepper

1 small leg of lamb with the aitchbone removed
(about 5 pounds without the bone, see Note)

1 pound thinly sliced pancetta

1 large yellow onion, coarsely chopped (1¼ cups)

1 large carrot, peeled and coarsely chopped (½ cup)

1 large rib celery, trimmed and cut into 1-inch pieces (½ cup)

2 cups dry white wine, such as Pinot Grigio or Trebbiano

Preheat the oven to 375°F. In a food processor, combine the anchovies, garlic, thyme, rosemary, orange zest, and olive oil and process into a smooth paste. Season to taste with salt and pepper.

Using a small paring knife, make 1½-inch-deep slits all over the lamb. Spread the herb paste all over the lamb, working it into the slits; season the lamb with salt and pepper.

On a large sheet of plastic wrap or waxed paper, overlap the pancetta slices to form a 12- x 15-inch rectangle. Set the lamb on the pancetta and wrap the plastic around the leg, pressing to help the pancetta adhere. Peel off the plastic and reposition any slices of pancetta that have moved. Using seven or eight long pieces of kitchen string, tie the roast at 1-inch intervals.

Scatter the onion, carrot, and celery in the bottom of a roasting pan just large enough to hold the lamb and lay the meat on top. Roast for 1 hour 40 minutes to 2 hours until the pancetta is golden and an instant-read thermometer inserted in the center of the thickest part of the meat registers 140°F to 145°F. For medium-rare cook to 135°F. Transfer the lamb to a cutting board, tent it loosely with aluminum foil, and let it rest for 20 minutes.

Meanwhile, set the roasting pan over high heat. Pour in the wine and bring the liquid to a boil, scraping up any browned bits from the bottom of the pan. Strain it into a small saucepan, pressing on the vegetables to extract as much liquid as possible. Discard the vegetables. Skim the fat from the surface and boil until the sauce is reduced to 1 cup, about 20 minutes, then pour it into a gravy boat. Remove the kitchen string from the lamb and cut the meat across the grain into thin slices. Serve at once with the sauce.

Note: The aitchbone refers to the back section of an animal's pelvic bone. It should be removed before you buy the roast. Anyone in the meat department can do this. When this bone is removed from the leg, the meat cooks more evenly.

Tagliata di Manzo
Sliced Steak with Rosemary

[MAKES 4 SERVINGS]

This is the quintessential steak to savor anytime you want the great taste of beef. Serve it Tuscan-style with white beans scented with fresh sage or Rosemary Roasted Potatoes (page 193).

Four 14-ounce prime beef strip steaks, about 1½ inches thick

¼ cup extra-virgin olive oil

2 tablespoons Rosemary Salt (page 253) or sea salt with a pinch of dried or minced fresh rosemary leaves added

1 lemon, cut in half

Heat a charcoal or gas barbecue or stovetop grill until hot. Position the grids about 4 inches from the heat. Rub the steaks liberally with 2 tablespoons of the olive oil and generously season with Rosemary Salt.

Grill the steaks over high heat until they reach the desired degree of doneness, about 5 minutes per side for rare, or 7 to 8 minutes for medium-rare. Transfer the steaks to a cutting board, tent them lightly with aluminum foil, and let them rest for 5 to 10 minutes to allow the juices to be reabsorbed into the meat. Cut each steak crosswise into ¾-inch thick slices and transfer to warm plates. Drizzle with lemon juice and serve at once.

Carré di Agnello con Rapini e Patate con Salsa al Vino Rosso
Roasted Rack of Lamb with Broccoli Rabe and Potatoes and Red Wine Sauce

[MAKES 4 SERVINGS]

For celebrations, rack of lamb is an indulgent, deliciously tender cut of meat. I prefer to roast the racks until the meat is medium-rare, then I serve the chops with a simple pan sauce. Ask the butcher to remove the chine bone (the remaining section of the backbone) from the racks if it has not been done, so that when cooked you can easily cut them into individual chops.

¼ cup lightly toasted bread crumbs

2 cloves garlic, minced

1 teaspoon chopped fresh thyme leaves

1 teaspoon chopped fresh rosemary leaves

3 tablespoons olive oil, plus extra for brushing

2 well-trimmed, frenched racks of lamb with the chine bone removed (about 1½ pounds trimmed weight without the chine bone)

Sea salt and freshly ground black pepper

Broccoli Rabe and Potatoes (recipe follows)

For the Sauce

4 teaspoons extra-virgin olive oil

2 tablespoons minced shallots

1 teaspoon minced garlic

½ cup dry red wine, such as Chianti or Barbera

continued

169

2 cups Veal Stock (page 258) or Rich Chicken Stock (page 256)

2 teaspoons chopped fresh thyme leaves

2 teaspoons chopped fresh rosemary leaves

Sea salt and freshly ground black pepper

1 tablespoon cold butter

Preheat the oven to 450°F. In a small bowl, combine the bread crumbs, garlic, thyme, rosemary, and oil and stir to blend.

Brush the lamb racks all over with a little oil. Heat a roasting pan over medium-high heat until hot. Add the racks, flesh side down, and sear them for 3 to 4 minutes until nicely browned.

Turn the racks over and season liberally with salt and pepper to taste. Let stand for 1 to 2 minutes to cool slightly, then pat the bread crumb mixture on the flesh side. Cover the tips of the bones with aluminum foil, if desired, and roast the rack, flesh side up, for 12 to 15 minutes for medium-rare to medium. An instant-read thermometer inserted into the meatiest part of the roast should measure 125°F for medium-rare and 130°F for medium.

Meanwhile, prepare the Broccoli Rabe and Potatoes and the sauce.

Once the lamb is done, remove the racks from the oven and let them rest for 10 minutes before carving.

For the Sauce:

Heat the olive oil in a 1-quart saucepan over medium-high heat for about 1 minute. Add the shallots and cook, stirring, until translucent, about 1 minute. Stir in the garlic and cook until fragrant, about 30 seconds. Pour in the red wine and bring the liquid to a boil over high heat. Cook until the liquid has almost completely evaporated, 1 to 2 minutes.

Stir in the veal stock, thyme, and rosemary. Return the liquid to a boil and reduce it over high heat until it reaches a sauce consistency, 15 to 20 minutes. Season with salt and pepper to taste. Pour the sauce through a fine strainer into a small pan. Whisk in the cold butter and keep warm over low heat.

To serve, cut the racks into individual chops and place 4 chops on each dinner plate. Divide the broccoli rabe and potatoes among the plates, spoon the sauce over the lamb, and serve.

Rapine e Patate
Broccoli Rabe and Potatoes

Sea salt

One 12-ounce bunch broccoli rabe, coarse stems and leaves trimmed
and discarded, cut into small pieces

2 cups fingerling or new potatoes, peeled and cut into ½-inch cubes

2 tablespoons pine nuts

3 tablespoons olive oil

3 cloves garlic, crushed

½ teaspoon red pepper flakes

Freshly ground black pepper

Bring a large pot of generously salted water to a boil. Add the broccoli rabe, bring the water back to a boil, and cook for 2 to 3 minutes more. Drain the broccoli rabe, transfer it to a large bowl of ice water to cool, then drain well and set aside.

In another pot, cover the potatoes with cold, salted water and bring to a boil. Once the water boils, cook for 1 to 2 minutes, drain in a colander, and set aside.

Put the pine nuts in a small skillet in a single layer. Lightly toast them over medium-low heat until lightly browned, 3 to 4 minutes, shaking the pan often to prevent burning. Alternatively, toast them in a toaster oven heated to 350°F for the same length of time, shaking the pan often. Set aside.

Heat the olive oil in a large heavy skillet over medium heat. Add the garlic and pepper flakes and cook, stirring, until the garlic is golden, 30 seconds to 1 minute. Reduce the heat to medium-low, add the broccoli rabe and potatoes, and stir to combine. Cook, stirring occasionally, until the broccoli rabe and potatoes are heated through and the stems are tender, about 4 minutes. Season to taste with salt and pepper. Add the pine nuts and stir to blend.

Brasato di Manzo
Braised Short Ribs

[MAKES 4 SERVINGS]

Italians have a passion for slowly braised, fork-tender meats, like shanks and pot roasts. While butchers in Italy don't traditionally cut beef short ribs, these meaty rectangles, gently simmered in wine and beef stock, really fit the bill for comfort fare in any country. The meatiest short ribs are "plate cut," cut from along the ribs, not crosswise. Polenta would be the perfect partner for the luscious meat.

As a final garnish, top the meat with a little freshly grated horseradish. It perfumes the meat and adds just a touch of heat to complement the hearty flavors. It will be a revelation compared with the bottled variety, which tends to be vinegary and sour.

4 large plate-cut short ribs of beef, about 10 ounces each, about 2½ x 5 inches long, patted dry with paper towels

Sea salt and freshly ground black pepper

2 tablespoons canola or other vegetable oil

1 medium-large yellow onion, chopped (1 cup)

1 large carrot, peeled and chopped (½ cup)

1 large rib celery, trimmed and chopped (½ cup)

One 28-ounce can diced Italian tomatoes, undrained

1 bottle hearty red wine, such as Chianti or Sangiovese

3 bay leaves

2 sprigs fresh rosemary

4 to 6 cups beef or Veal Stock (page 258), to cover meat

Freshly grated horseradish

Liberally season the short ribs with salt and pepper. In a large, heavy-bottomed casserole or Dutch oven just large enough to hold the short ribs in a single layer, heat the oil over high heat until almost smoking, add the short ribs and brown on all sides, about 10 minutes total cooking time. Do this in batches, if necessary, so the meat is not crowded and the oil remains hot and sizzles with each addition. Remove the short ribs to a bowl and set aside. Discard all but 2 tablespoons of fat.

Add the onion, carrot, and celery and cook, stirring, until the onion begins to soften, 2 to 3 minutes. Add the tomatoes, wine, bay leaves, and rosemary and scrape up all the browned bits. Return the short ribs to the pot and pour in enough stock just to cover them. Bring the liquid to a boil, then reduce the heat to a gentle simmer, cover, and cook until the meat is very tender and falling off the bone, 2½ to 3 hours.

Transfer the short ribs to a serving platter and tent with aluminum foil. Skim the fat from the surface of the braising liquid, then pour it through a fine strainer it into a saucepan, pressing on the vegetables to extract as much liquid as possible. Discard the vegetables. Cook the liquid over high heat until it is reduced to about 2 cups. If needed, return the short ribs to the liquid to reheat. Serve the short ribs with freshly grated horseradish on top.

Bollito Misto
Assorted Boiled Meats

[MAKES 6 TO 8 GENEROUS SERVINGS
WITH LEFTOVERS]

B*ollito misto* is a traditional Piemontese dish
that has withstood changing tastes and the passage of time. Although "mixed boiled dinner" sounds like
pedestrian fare, it has countless fans. The dish includes a variety of meats and vegetables,
with every ingredient meant to complement the others. It is always served with condiments like
Green Sauce (page 261) and Cremona-Style *Mostarda* (page 263).
The intense sauces accent the somewhat mild meats.
For my version, I use beef, veal, veal tongue (which is optional), roasting chicken,
and fresh pork sausage, or *cotechino,* that is a specialty of Emilia-Romagna.
Bollito misto is served on a heated platter and everyone helps himself or
herself. The sharing makes for a genial dining experience.

Sea salt

3 medium ribs celery, trimmed and cut into large chunks

2 medium carrots, peeled and cut into large chunks

2 medium-large yellow onions, stuck with 2 cloves each

2 pounds beef cut from the shoulder, cut into two 1-pound pieces

2 pounds breast of veal, cut in half

One 3½- to 4-pound capon or chicken, excess fat trimmed, cut in half lengthwise

One ¾-pound *cotechino* or garlic sausage (see Sources, page 266)

One 1-pound veal tongue (optional)

Freshly ground black pepper

Coarse sea salt

Green Sauce (page 261)

Cremona-Style *Mostarda* (page 263)

Fill a large pot with 8 quarts lightly salted water. Add the celery, carrots, and onions and bring the liquid to a rolling boil. Add the beef, reduce the heat so the liquid is simmering, and cook uncovered for 1 hour. Add the veal and capon or chicken, and simmer for about 1 hour more until all the meats are fork tender. Prick the *cotechino* sausage liberally and add it to the cooked meats to let it heat through, about 10 minutes.

If using the tongue, at the same time as you start cooking the beef, fill a second pot with 4 quarts lightly salted water and bring to a boil. Add the tongue, reduce the heat so the liquid is simmering, and cook until it is fork tender, about 2 hours. Remove and, when cool enough to handle, peel the tongue.

To serve, cut the tongue and *cotechino* into thick slices. Arrange all of the meats on a heated platter. Sprinkle with coarse salt, if desired, and with some of the hot broth ladled over the pieces. Carve the meats at the table and pass the Green Sauce and *Mostarda*.

Stufato di Capriolo alla Süd Tirolese
South Tyrolean Venison Stew

[MAKES 4 SERVINGS]

The Süd Tirol—the Alto Adige in Italian—
is in northeastern Italy. Once part of Austria, it was annexed to Italy after World War I. The area
includes the soaring Dolomites and hauntingly beautiful alpine vistas. The food is hearty enough
to nourish the many hikers and skiers who travel these paths. This hearty venison stew reflects influences
from the area's Austrian neighbors, where game meats are staples. Dark red venison is very lean.
To seal in the meat's juices, lightly floured pieces are sautéed over high heat
to form a golden crust, then gently simmered in liquid. Serve the stew over soft polenta.
I prefer to season foods with salt and pepper first, then dredge them in flour, rather than combining
the steps, because the pieces are more evenly coated this way.

3 tablespoons olive oil

2 pounds well-trimmed venison stew meat,
   cut into 1½-inch pieces (See Sources, page 266)

Sea salt and freshly ground black pepper

¼ cup all-purpose flour

2 medium-large yellow onions, chopped (2 cups)

2 large carrots, peeled and chopped (1 cup)

2 large ribs celery, trimmed and chopped (1 cup)

1 ripe tomato, peeled (see page 105), seeded, and chopped (1 cup),
   or substitute drained, diced canned tomatoes

2 cloves garlic, crushed

4 tablespoons tomato paste

1 tablespoon chopped fresh thyme leaves, plus a few sprigs for garnish

continued

1 tablespoon chopped fresh sage

½ tablespoon juniper berries, bruised

2 bay leaves

2 cups hearty dry red wine, such as Sangiovese

3 cups Rich Chicken Stock (page 256) or beef stock

Heat the olive oil in a large pot over high heat. Meanwhile, in a mixing bowl, season the venison with salt and pepper, turning to coat it evenly, then repeat with the flour, patting to remove any excess. When the oil is very hot, slowly add the pieces of meat in a single layer so the oil remains hot and sizzles with each addition. Cook the venison on all sides, turning occasionally, until golden brown and crusty, 2 to 3 minutes. If the pot is too small, do this in batches, cooking as many pieces as will fit comfortably in the bottom of the pan. Remove the cooked cubes to a bowl.

When all the venison is browned, add the onions, carrots, and celery to the pan and cook, stirring occasionally, until limp, about 5 minutes. Stir in the tomato, garlic, tomato paste, thyme, sage, juniper berries, and bay leaves and cook for 1 to 2 minutes. Season with salt and pepper.

Pour in the red wine and bring the liquid to a boil over high heat, stirring up all the browned bits on the bottom of the pan. Cook until it is reduced by half. Add the venison to the pot. Pour in the stock and bring the liquid to a boil. Cover and reduce the heat so the liquid is just simmering. Cook for 45 minutes to 1 hour, until the meat is very tender. Serve at once or let cool and refrigerate in a covered container. Gently reheat before serving.

le verdure

Cavoletti con *Pancetta* Brussels Sprouts with Pancetta *Scarola con Acciughe* Savory Escarole with Anchovies *Cavolo Nero alla Toscana* Tuscan Braised Kale *Spinaci alla Contadina* Farmer-Style Spinach *Piselli con Prosciutto* Peas with Prosciutto *Finocchio Arrosto con Parmigiano-Reggiano* Roasted Fennel with Parmigiano-Reggiano *Patate al Forno con Rosmarino* Rosemary Roasted Potatoes *Funghi al Forno* Oven-Roasted Mushrooms

VEGETABLES

Cavoletti con Pancetta
Brussels Sprouts with Pancetta

[MAKES 4 SERVINGS]

If every child and grown-up who claims not to like Brussels sprouts tasted this version of the vegetable, I'm sure they would change their mind. The little heads are cut in half, rather than boiled whole, to release their inherent sweetness. Sautéing and oven-roasting them also reduces their bitterness as they gently caramelize. When I came back to America, the first vegetable I cooked for my family was roasted Brussels sprouts. You don't need any stock or liquid in the pan because the leaves hold moisture.

2 tablespoons olive oil

2 tablespoons unsalted butter

3 ounces pancetta, cut into small cubes

1 pound Brussels sprouts, bruised outer leaves discarded, trimmed and halved

Sea salt and freshly ground black pepper

2 cloves garlic, crushed

Preheat the oven to 400°F.

Combine the oil and butter in a large ovenproof skillet and heat over medium heat. Add the pancetta and cook, stirring occasionally, until it begins to crisp, about 3 minutes. Add the Brussels sprouts and cook, shaking the pan occasionally, until they begin to brown, about 5 minutes. Season to taste with salt and pepper. Transfer the pan to the oven and roast, shaking the pan occasionally, until the Brussels sprouts are brown on all sides, 15 to 20 minutes, depending on size. Add the garlic and roast for 5 minutes more. Serve as a side dish.

Spinaci alla Contadina
Farmer-Style Spinach

[MAKES 4 SERVINGS]

Farmer-style spinach combines sautéed mushrooms, balsamic vinegar, and white wine for a savory vegetable dish. Like most Italian vegetables, it is well cooked and tender.

¼ cup extra-virgin olive oil

1 small yellow onion, chopped (½ cup)

2 cloves garlic, chopped

1 pound white mushrooms, stems trimmed, wiped, and thickly sliced

1½ pounds fresh spinach with coarse steams removed, washed and cut into thick ribbons

2 tablespoons balsamic vinegar

½ cup dry white wine, such as Pinot Grigio

Sea salt and freshly ground black pepper

Finely chopped flat-leaf parsley, for garnish

Heat the olive oil in a large heavy skillet over medium-high heat. Add the onion and garlic and cook, stirring, until the onion starts to soften, 3 to 4 minutes. Stir in the mushrooms and cook, stirring, until they begin to color, 3 to 4 minutes. Add the spinach and cook, stirring continuously, until it is wilted, 2 to 3 minutes.

Stir in the vinegar and cook over high heat, stirring occasionally, until it evaporates, 1 to 2 minutes. Add the white wine, reduce the heat to medium, and simmer, stirring occasionally, until the wine has almost completely evaporated, about 10 minutes. Season to taste with salt and pepper, sprinkle with parsley, and serve as a side dish.

Piselli con Prosciutto
Peas with Prosciutto

[MAKES 4 SERVINGS]

Peas are a popular vegetable that both Italians and Italian-Americans often prepare with a little prosciutto to balance their sweet taste. In my version, a couple of tablespoons of butter and a few drops of water swirled into the pan just before serving blend the flavors and add a nice glaze.

2 tablespoons extra-virgin olive oil

1 small yellow onion, finely chopped (½ cup)

3 cloves garlic, minced

1 pound shelled fresh spring peas, blanched, or
   one 10-ounce package frozen petite peas, defrosted

1 sprig fresh thyme

Sea salt and freshly ground black pepper

3 ounces prosciutto, finely chopped

2 tablespoons unsalted butter

Heat the oil in a large heavy skillet over medium-low heat. Add the onion and garlic and cook, stirring, until the onion is tender, 3 to 4 minutes. Stir in the peas and thyme, season with salt and pepper to taste, and stew until the peas are tender, 10 to 12 minutes if fresh, or 5 minutes if frozen. Add the prosciutto and cook, stirring occasionally, for 1 to 2 minutes. Stir in the butter and about ½ teaspoon of hot water, swirl for a few seconds, taste to adjust the seasonings, and serve as a side dish.

Finocchio Arrosto con Parmigiano-Reggiano
Roasted Fennel with
Parmigiano-Reggiano

[MAKES 4 SERVINGS]

Cooked fennel is popular in antipasti and vegetable side dishes. When baked or roasted, its somewhat assertive anise flavor mellows. It is a delicious partner for the Parmigiano cheese and bread crumb topping with hints of rosemary.

2 medium-large bulbs fennel, trimmed, cored, and
  cut vertically into thick slices

1½ to 2 teaspoons Rosemary Salt (page 253) or sea salt with a pinch
  of dried or minced fresh rosemary leaves added

Freshly ground black pepper

2 cloves garlic, minced

⅓ cup freshly grated Parmigiano-Reggiano cheese

⅓ cup lightly toasted bread crumbs

2 tablespoons olive oil

1 tablespoon minced fresh rosemary leaves

Preheat the oven to 375°F. Lightly oil the bottom of a 9- x 13- x 2-inch baking dish.

Lay the slices of fennel in the prepared baking dish, season with Rosemary Salt and plenty of black pepper, and sprinkle on the garlic. Combine the cheese and bread crumbs and sprinkle evenly over the fennel. Drizzle the olive oil over the top and sprinkle on the rosemary. Bake until the fennel is fork tender and the top is golden brown, 45 minutes to 1 hour. Serve as a side dish.

Patate al Forno con Rosmarino
Rosemary Roasted Potatoes

[MAKES 4 SERVINGS]

In my version of roasted potatoes, minced rosemary and garlic are added at the last minute and just warmed through, giving a big bang of fresh flavor as you eat them.

2 pounds small red potatoes, scrubbed and cut into small chunks

4 tablespoons extra-virgin olive oil

2 tablespoons fresh rosemary leaves

2 cloves garlic

Coarse sea salt

Preheat the oven to 375°F. Line a large sheet pan with aluminum foil. Toss the potatoes with 2 tablespoons of the olive oil, spread them evenly on the sheet pan, and bake, turning occasionally with a spatula, until golden brown on the outside and creamy inside, about 30 minutes.

While the potatoes are roasting, finely chop the rosemary and garlic together. Remove the pan from the oven and place it on top of the stove. Drizzle the remaining 2 tablespoons of olive oil over the potatoes, sprinkle with sea salt and 2 tablespoons of the rosemary-garlic mixture, and turn to mix well and heat the seasonings through. Serve at once as a side dish.

dolci

Granita di Limone Lemon Granita with Fresh Strawberry Sauce Semifreddo alla Vaniglia con Conserva di Ananas Vanilla Semifreddo with Pineapple Compote Pesche Arrosto con Strudel Roasted Peaches with Streusel Topping Albicocche Arrosto con Vin Santo, Zabaglione e Mandorle Candite Vanilla-Roasted Apricots with Vin Santo, Zabaglione, and Candied Almonds Budino al Limone con Marmellata di Mirtilli Steamed Lemon Pudding with Berry Marmalade Budini di Zucca con Marmellata di Frutta Secca Steamed Pumpkin Puddings with Dried Fruit Marmalade Biscotti Ripieni Vanilla Cookies with Chocolate Buttercream Filling Tortino di Mele Crustless Apple Tart Crochette di Ricotta con Salsa di Cioccolato Ricotta Beignets with Chocolate Dipping Sauce Crostata di Limone con Marmellata di Mirtilli Lemon Tart with Berry Marmalade Pasticcino di Cioccolato con Lampone Individual Chocolate Cakes with Fresh Raspberries Gelato alla Vaniglia Affogato in Caffè Vanilla Ice Cream with Coffee Shots Tartine di Ciliege al Mascarpone Individual Cherry Mascarpone Tartlets Torta di Mandorle e Albicocche alla Crema Almond Cake with Roasted Apricots and Vanilla Cream Crespelle di Nutella con Gelato alla Vaniglia e Nocciole Nutella-Filled Crêpes with Vanilla Gelato and Salted Hazelnuts Coppa di Tiramisù Tiramisù Cup Gelato alla Vaniglia Vanilla Bean Gelato Gelato al Miele Millefiori Wildflower Honey Gelato Gelato alle More Blackberry Gelato Moca Gelato Mocha Gelato Gelato di Yogurt alla Vaniglia Vanilla Frozen Yogurt Trio di Sorbetti Sorbet Trio: Rhubarb Sorbet, Mango Sorbet, Green Apple Sorbet

Granita di Limone
Lemon Granita with Fresh Strawberry Sauce

[MAKES 8 SERVINGS]

Granitas are made with frozen sweetened fruit juices that are stirred while chilling. The icy desserts have a granular texture that can't be scooped into perfect snowballs. A popular street food in Italy, they are sold in little cone-shaped paper cups. By far, the most popular flavor is lemon. This tangy lemon granita, served in tall glasses with fresh strawberry sauce and mint leaves, is my play on those snow cones. As they are being served, a little fizzy Moscato d'Asti is poured over the dessert. I serve them with Vanilla Cookies with Chocolate Buttercream Filling (page 215).

4 cups freshly squeezed lemon juice (about 24 medium lemons), plus grated zest of 2 lemons (about 2 teaspoons)

3 cups sugar

4 pints fresh strawberries, stemmed, hulled, and quartered (about 10 cups cut berries), plus berries for garnish

Fresh mint leaves, for garnish

2 cups Moscato d'Asti (see sidebar)

Combine the lemon juice and zest with 1½ cups of the sugar in a medium-size saucepan and bring to a boil over high heat, gently stirring occasionally. Cook until the sugar is dissolved, about 5 minutes. Remove the pan from the heat, cover with plastic wrap to prevent sugar crystals from forming, and let the liquid stand for at least 20 minutes for the flavors to infuse.

Strain through a sieve into a deep metal pan, such as a loaf pan, and freeze for at least 3 hours, stirring with a fork every half hour and scraping the ice crystals from the edges, until solid.

While the granita is freezing, combine the strawberries, the remaining 1½ cups of sugar, and

The day before you plan to serve the semifreddo, sprinkle the gelatin over 3 tablespoons water in a small bowl and set aside until the liquid is absorbed and the gelatin softens, about 5 minutes. Combine the egg yolks and whole egg in a large bowl and beat with an electric mixer until pale yellow and thick, 4 to 5 minutes. Combine 6 tablespoons of the sugar and 2 tablespoons water in a small saucepan and bring to a rolling boil over high heat, then cook for 3 minutes without stirring. Whisk the gelatin into the egg mixture, then gradually pour in the sugar syrup, beating constantly. Continue to beat until cool, about 10 minutes.

Stir the yogurt and vanilla seeds together in a small bowl. Fold the yogurt into the egg mixture, then fold in the whipped cream. Pour the mixture into individual ⅓-cup molds, custard cups, or a cupcake pan lined with plastic wrap or cupcake liners and freeze overnight until solid.

Purée half of the pineapple in an electric blender until smooth. Reserve in the refrigerator until ready to use.

Combine the remaining 8 tablespoons of sugar, the star anise, and ¼ cup water in a small heavy saucepan. Bring to a rolling boil over high heat, then cook for 3 minutes without stirring. Strain the syrup into a bowl, stir in the rum, and let it cool slightly. Stir in the remaining diced pineapple, then chill until cold.

To serve, let the semifreddos soften for 15 minutes. Divide the pineapple purée among 6 flat soup bowls. To unmold the semifreddos, run a knife around the edge of the mold with a sharp knife or peel off the cupcake liners and put one in each bowl. Spoon on the pineapple compote, sprinkle on a few tarragon leaves, and serve.

Pesche Arrosto con Strudel
Roasted Peaches with Streusel Topping

[MAKES 8 SERVINGS]

For this dessert, ripe golden peaches are roasted to intensify their taste, then topped with crunchy streusel and vanilla gelato. The tastes and textures really dance on your tongue. Look for locally grown, seasonal peaches that smell peachy. Once picked, the fruit won't ripen any further.

1 cup all-purpose flour

¾ cup light brown sugar

2 teaspoons baking soda

1 teaspoon baking powder

1 teaspoon salt

½ pound (2 sticks) cold unsalted butter, cut in small pieces

8 firm ripe freestone peaches, cut in half, pits removed

1 vanilla bean, split lengthwise and seeds scraped, or
    1 tablespoon vanilla extract

½ cup sugar

¼ cup peach schnapps or liqueur

1 quart Vanilla Bean Gelato (page 240) or store-bought gelato

In the bowl of a food processor, combine the flour, brown sugar, baking soda, baking powder, and salt and pulse to blend. Add the butter and pulse until the mixture resembles coarse meal. Do not allow it to form a ball. Remove the dough, sprinkle it onto a flat baking pan lined with parchment or aluminum foil, and refrigerate for at least 1 hour or until firm.

Meanwhile, preheat the oven to 325°F.

Bake the streusel until browned, 14 to 16 minutes. Remove and cool completely, then break it into small pieces. Leave the oven on.

While the streusel is cooking, lay the peaches cut side down in a shallow baking pan. Cut the vanilla bean into 4 pieces. Combine the sugar, the vanilla bean and seeds, the schnapps, and ¼ cup of water in a bowl and pour over the peaches.

Bake at 325°F until tender, 10 to 12 minutes. Baking times will vary depending on the ripeness of the peaches and can even take longer than 12 minutes. Remove, take out the vanilla bean, and set the peaches aside to cool in the liquid.

To serve, divide the peaches and their liquid among 8 plates. Scoop a small ball of gelato into each half, spoon some streusel over the gelato, and serve.

Save Used Vanilla Beans

Once you scrape the seeds from a vanilla bean—even if you have cooked with it—save it to make vanilla sugar. Pat it dry, if necessary, then put the bean into a container and cover it with sugar. Vanilla-flavored sugar lasts indefinitely. Sprinkle some over summer fruits as they roast or stir it into your coffee.

Albicocche Arrosto con Vin Santo, Zabaglione e Mandorle Candite
Vanilla-Roasted Apricots with Vin Santo, Zabaglione, and Candied Almonds

[MAKES 4 SERVINGS]

I still remember my first discovery of fresh apricots, with their floral perfume-like taste. To my surprise, once I cracked the pit inside the fruit, there was something that looked like an almond. When tasted, it was bitter but indeed almondesque. Since then I have always appreciated the affinity between apricots and almonds. They are partnered here with a warm, custard-like zabaglione. Rather than using the traditional Marsala, I like the way honey-almond-tasting Vin Santo brings all of the zabaglione's flavors together. This makes more sauce than you need for this recipe. Cover and refrigerate the leftovers for up to three days. Serve it with fresh fruit or over cake.

½ cup slivered almonds, lightly toasted

1 large egg white

¾ cup sugar

6 apricots, halved and pitted

1 vanilla bean

½ cup orange liqueur or fresh orange juice

½ cup heavy cream

4 large egg yolks

Pinch of salt

6 tablespoons Vin Santo (see sidebar)

Fresh thyme leaves, for garnish

Preheat the oven to 250°F.

Combine the almonds and egg white in a bowl, toss to coat evenly, then pour into a strainer to drain the excess egg. Put ¼ cup of the sugar into a small bowl, add the almonds, and stir to coat evenly. Spread the almonds on a baking sheet and cook, stirring often with a wooden spoon, for 20 to 25 minutes, or until dry. Remove, transfer to another tray, and cool completely.

Increase the temperature to 325°F. Lay the apricots face down in an oven-safe dish. Split the vanilla bean down the center and scrape out the seeds. Stir the seeds of the vanilla bean and orange liqueur together in a small bowl, then pour over the apricots. Cut the scraped vanilla bean into 6 pieces and add to the fruit. Bake the apricots until very tender, 10 to 15 minutes depending on the ripeness of the fruit.

In a medium-size bowl, whip the heavy cream into soft peaks and set aside. In a medium-size metal bowl, whisk together the egg yolks, the remaining ½ cup of sugar, the salt, and Vin Santo. Place the bowl over a pot of simmering water (the bottom of the bowl should not be touching the water) and whisk continuously until the mixture triples in volume and is warm to the touch, about 5 minutes. Remove the bowl from the heat, place it in a bowl of ice water, and whisk until the zabaglione is cold. Fold in the reserved whipped cream.

Divide the apricots among 4 shallow bowls. Top each with 2 tablespoons of Vin Santo zabaglione, sprinkle with candied almonds, garnish with a piece of vanilla bean and a few thyme leaves, and serve.

Vin Santo

Vin Santo, or "holy wine," is a sweet Tuscan dessert wine often served with biscotti for dipping into it. The amber-colored wine is made from Trebbiano and white Malvasia grapes that are hung on beams or straw mats to dry. They are then barrel aged for three to ten years. The wine can be aged for decades, during which time its rich, floral bouquet and taste intensify.

Budino al Limone con Marmellata di Mirtilli
Steamed Lemon Pudding with Berry Marmalade

Serve this lemony-sweet, soft and airy dessert as a flavorful light finale to the grandest dinner. As the pudding bakes, the juices settle at the bottom. The cooked puddings are inverted before serving, revealing a beautiful, shiny lemon gelée on top.

Vegetable cooking spray

½ cup sugar, plus extra for dusting molds (about ½ teaspoon each)

¾ cup buttermilk

6 tablespoons freshly squeezed lemon juice
(about 2 large lemons), plus grated zest of 1 lemon

2 extra large eggs, separated

¼ cup all-purpose flour, sifted

¼ teaspoon salt

1 cup Berry Marmalade (page 223)

Preheat the oven to 325°F. Spray six ½-cup aluminum cups, soufflé dishes, or ½-cup muffin tins with vegetable cooking spray and dust lightly with sugar.

In a large bowl, whisk together the buttermilk, the remaining ½ cup of sugar, lemon juice and zest, egg yolks, and flour until completely smooth. In another bowl, beat the egg whites and salt into soft peaks, about 3 minutes. Gently fold the whites into the lemon mixture. Do not overmix.

Pour the lemon mixture into the cups, filling them almost to the top. Put them in a deep baking dish and pour 1 inch of hot water into the bottom of the baking dish. Cover the pan with aluminum foil and bake for 20 minutes. Remove the foil and bake for 10 to 15 minutes more until the tops are puffed and the edges are pulling away from the sides of the molds. Remove and cool for 20 minutes.

To unmold, run a knife around the edges and invert onto dessert plates. Serve each *budino* with 2 to 3 tablespoons of Berry Marmalade spooned over it.

Budini di Zucca con Marmellata di Frutta Secca
Steamed Pumpkin Puddings with Dried Fruit Marmalade

Although Italians don't usually celebrate Thanksgiving, anyone in America or Italy would be pleased to serve these beautiful, individually steamed puddings for our favorite holiday, or for any autumn meal. They are is dressed up with a dried fruit marmalade and sweetened vanilla-scented mascarpone cheese.

Budini

1 tablespoon unsalted butter

½ cup granulated sugar, plus 2 tablespoons extra for dusting ramekins

2 cups light brown sugar

1½ cups pumpkin purée (almost all of one 15-ounce can)

9 large eggs, separated

¾ cup all-purpose flour

1 teaspoon ground cinnamon

½ teaspoon ground nutmeg

⅛ teaspoon ground cloves

3 cups buttermilk

Pinch of salt

Dried Fruit Marmalade

½ cup dried figs (about 6), cut in 6 pieces

½ cup dried apricots (about 15), quartered

½ cup dried cranberries

½ cup golden raisins

continued

2 cups cranberry juice

1 vanilla bean, split lengthwise and seeds scraped, or
   1 tablespoon vanilla extract

Sweet Mascarpone

One 17-ounce container mascarpone cheese

¼ cup confectioners' sugar

1 vanilla bean, split lengthwise and seeds scraped, or
   1 tablespoon vanilla extract

Dried apple chips, for garnish (optional)

To make the Budini:

Preheat the oven to 350°F. Butter twelve 6-ounce ramekins or custard cups and dust with 2 tablespoons of the sugar.

In a large bowl, whisk together the ½ cup of granulated sugar, the brown sugar, pumpkin purée, egg yolks, flour, cinnamon, nutmeg, and clove until combined. Add the buttermilk and whisk until completely smooth. In a medium-size bowl, beat the egg whites and salt into soft peaks with an electric mixer, about 5 minutes. Gently fold the egg whites into the batter until evenly incorporated.

Pour the batter into the prepared cups. Place them in a wide pan large enough to hold them comfortably and pour 1 inch of hot water into the bottom of the pan. Cover the cups with aluminum foil and bake for about 15 minutes. Remove the aluminum foil and continue baking for another 8 to 10 minutes or until they have risen slightly and are lightly browned on top. Remove the cups from the water bath and set on a rack to cool.

While the puddings are baking, make the Dried Fruit Marmalade:

Combine the figs, apricots, cranberries, raisins, cranberry juice, and the vanilla bean and seeds or the vanilla extract in a medium-size nonreactive saucepan over medium heat. Bring to a boil and cook, stirring, until the dried fruit is plump and the liquid has reduced slightly, about 15 minutes. Remove the vanilla bean, if using. Set the marmalade aside and keep warm.

For the Sweet Mascarpone:

Combine the mascarpone cheese, confectioners' sugar, and vanilla seeds or extract in a medium-size bowl and stir until well incorporated.

While still warm, invert the puddings onto a large platter and let them cool to room temperature. Serve them on individual plates with 3 tablespoons of marmalade. Top the marmalade with a generous dollop of mascarpone, and garnish with a dried apple chip, if desired.

Biscotti Ripieni
Vanilla Cookies with Chocolate Buttercream Filling

[MAKES ABOUT 18 FILLED COOKIES]

For years, my mom and I were always trying out recipes in an attempt to recreate the butter sandwich cookies we bought in the Jewish bakeries near where we lived. This recipe is the winner. They are similar to a popular sandwich cookie made by a well-known American company and named for the northern Italian city of Milano.

½ cup sugar

6 ounces (1½ sticks) unsalted butter

1 large egg

Grated zest of 1 navel orange

1¼ cups all-purpose flour

1 teaspoon salt

Buttercream

1 large egg white

¼ cup sugar

8 tablespoons (1 stick) unsalted butter, cut into small cubes and softened

½ teaspoon vanilla extract

½ cup bittersweet chocolate, chopped into small pieces

Preheat the oven to 325°F. Line a cookie sheet with parchment.

In a mixing bowl, cream the sugar and butter together until smooth. Stir in the egg and orange zest, then add the flour and salt, and stir together until smooth. You can also do this with an electric mixer, if desired. Transfer the dough to a pastry bag fitted with a medium-size plain tip, about ½

215

inch wide, and pipe thin strips about 2 inches long onto the pan, leaving about 2 inches between each strip. Bake in the lower third of the oven until lightly browned on the edges, 8 to 10 minutes. Remove with a spatula to a rack and let cool.

Meanwhile, prepare the Buttercream:
Combine the egg white and sugar in the top of a double boiler or a metal bowl that fits over a pan of simmering water. The bottom should not touch the water. Heat until the sugar is dissolved and the mixture is slightly thickened, whisking continuously.

Immediately remove the bowl from the water and begin beating the mixture with a hand-held electric mixer. Continue beating while slowly adding the butter. Beat until the mixture is room temperature and thickened, about the consistency of a thick confectioners' sugar-butter frosting, 10 to 15 minutes. About halfway through, the buttercream will look ugly. Keep beating; it will become smooth and thick. Beat in the vanilla. Cover and refrigerate for 10 to 20 minutes.

To assemble, place half of the cookies upside down (flat side up) on a sheet pan and spread each with a thin layer of buttercream. Top with the remaining cookies and refrigerate the tray until the buttercream sets, 10 to 15 minutes.

While the cookies are in the refrigerator, melt the chocolate in the top of a double boiler set over simmering water, stirring until smooth. Remove the inset and cool the chocolate to room temperature. Remove the cookies from the refrigerator. Holding each cookie by one end, dip half of it in the melted chocolate. Set it on a waxed-paper or parchment-lined tray. When all of the cookies are dipped, return them to the refrigerator for a few minutes to set.

Tortino di Mele
Crustless Apple Tart

[MAKES 8 SERVINGS]

This crustless, layered apple tart is especially tempting because it takes very little effort to make once the delicate Wildflower Honey Gelato is prepared. Tangy-sweet Granny Smith apples, liberally sprinkled with cinnamon sugar, steam until tender. When cooled, the tart is sliced into wedges with fresh berries and apple-caramel sauce drizzled on top. If you have a mandoline, this is a perfect opportunity to use it. If you can find fresh thyme flowers, or even sprigs of thyme, add them to give a final, unexpected but very exciting hint of flavor.

1¼ cups sugar

2 teaspoons ground cinnamon

5 tart green apples, such as Granny Smith, peeled, cored, and sliced about ⅛ inch thick

1 vanilla bean, split lengthwise and seeds scraped, or 1 tablespoon vanilla extract

1 cinnamon stick

1 cup apple juice

1 quart Wildflower Honey Gelato (see page 243) or store-bought vanilla, hazelnut, or other gelato

1 pint huckleberries or blueberries

Fresh thyme flowers or small thyme sprigs, for garnish (optional)

Preheat the oven to 325°F. Butter an 8-inch round cake pan.

Combine ¾ cup of the sugar and the ground cinnamon in a small bowl. Lay a thin layer of apples in the cake pan, slightly overlapping the slices, and sprinkle generously with cinnamon sugar. Continue adding layers of apples and sprinkling with cinnamon sugar until all the apples and sugar are used. Cover the pan with aluminum foil and bake until the apples are tender, about 1 hour 15 minutes. Remove and let cool completely.

Meanwhile, stir the remaining ½ cup of sugar and ¼ cup water together in a small, heavy-bottomed saucepan. Cook over medium heat without stirring until it is a rich dark brown, 4 to 5 minutes, watching carefully so that it does not burn. Add the vanilla bean and seeds, or vanilla extract, and cinnamon stick. Slowly and carefully whisk in the apple juice, bring the liquid to a boil, and cook over medium heat until reduced by a third, about 5 minutes. Remove the pan from the heat, cover with plastic wrap, infuse for at least 10 minutes, then pour through a fine strainer and cool.

To serve, slice the *tortino* in 8 pieces. Top each with a scoop of gelato. Divide the berries among the plates, spooning them around the *tortino*. Add a generous ribbon of apple-caramel sauce, garnish with thyme, if desired, and serve.

Crochette di Ricotta con Salsa di Cioccolato Ricotta Beignets with Chocolate Dipping Sauce

[MAKES 6 TO 8 SERVINGS]

Everyone seems to love fried dough in one form or another. At Italian fairs, the lines for crunchy *zepolle* or *crochette,* hot from a deep-fryer and dusted with confectioners' sugar, are always long.

Our guests are equally captivated with these lovely hot mouthfuls of dough. We serve them with rich chocolate, caramel, and berry sauces. The recipe for the chocolate sauce is below and the dessert is stupendous with that one alone. If you desire, prepare the Caramel Sauce on page 234 or buy a high-quality purchased sauce. For a berry sauce, purée and strain the Berry Marmalade on page 223. The secret to the beignet's extraordinarily soft yet meaty texture inside its inviting exterior is whole milk ricotta cheese. Crushed amaretti add a whisper of almond flavor, as well.

1 cup whole milk ricotta cheese

2 large eggs

¼ cup sugar

¼ cup all-purpose flour

¾ teaspoon baking powder

½ cup finely crushed amaretti cookies (about 16 cookies)

1 cup chopped bittersweet chocolate (5 ounces)

1 cup heavy cream

Vegetable oil, for deep-fat frying

Confectioners' sugar, for garnish

In a medium-size bowl, whisk the ricotta and eggs together until smooth. Add the sugar, flour, baking powder, and amaretti and stir until well blended. Cover and chill for at least 1 hour.

While the batter is chilling, put the chocolate in a small bowl. In a small saucepan, bring the heavy cream to a boil over medium-high heat, about 2 minutes. Remove the pan from the heat and pour the hot cream over the chopped chocolate, stirring until blended and smooth. Keep warm.

Fill a medium-size pot with at least 3 inches oil and heat until the oil measures about 360°F on a candy or instant-read thermometer. Carefully drop the *crochette* batter by the heaping tablespoon into the hot oil and cook, turning once, until brown on all sides, about 3 minutes. Using a slotted spoon, remove them from the oil and drain on paper towels. Dust with confectioners' sugar and serve immediately with chocolate sauce. If desired, serve with caramel and berry sauces, as well.

Crostata di Limone con Marmellata di Mirtilli
Lemon Tart with Berry Marmalade

[MAKES 8 SERVINGS]

This lovely lemon curd tart is an Italian favorite. The crust is delicate and slightly crumbly. (*Sablée* means "sandy" in French.) Blueberries and all berries love the tangy-sweet taste of lemon.

Sablée Dough

¾ cup confectioners' sugar

8 tablespoons (1 stick) unsalted butter, softened

Grated zest of 1 lemon

2 cups all-purpose flour, sifted

¼ teaspoon salt

1 large egg plus 1 large egg yolk

Lemon Curd

1½ cups fresh lemon juice (6 to 8 large lemons), plus thinly julienned zest of 2 lemons, for garnish

1 teaspoon powdered gelatin

4 large eggs

2 large egg yolks

1 cup sugar

¼ cup unsalted butter

Berry Marmalade

½ pint blackberries, cut in half

½ pint raspberries

½ pint blueberries

continued

2 tablespoons granulated sugar

1 tablespoon lemon juice

¼ cup berry jam

2 quarts Vanilla Frozen Yogurt (page 246) or store-bought
  whole milk vanilla yogurt

Fresh mint leaves, for garnish

To make the Sablée Dough:

In a large bowl, stir the sugar with the butter and lemon zest until blended. Add the flour and salt and stir just to incorporate. It will look like wet sand; do not overmix. Add the egg and stir until it comes together and begins to form a ball. Remove, pat into a thick disk, wrap in plastic wrap, and refrigerate until chilled, about 1 hour.

For the Lemon Curd:

Pour ¼ cup of the lemon juice into a small bowl. Sprinkle the gelatin over it and set aside to absorb the liquid and soften. Meanwhile, in a large metal bowl, whisk together the eggs, egg yolks, sugar, and remaining 1¼ cups of lemon juice. Place the bowl over a pot of simmering water, taking care that the insert does not touch the water. Cook, whisking continuously, until it thickens enough to coat the back of a wooden spoon, about 20 minutes.

Remove the bowl from the heat and whisk in the softened gelatin. Whisk in the butter until smooth, then pour the curd through a fine strainer into a clean bowl. Add the lemon zest, stir until slightly cooled, cover with plastic wrap, and set aside.

Preheat the oven to 325°F.

Unwrap the dough and put it on a lightly floured surface. With a lightly floured rolling pin, roll it into a circle about ¼ inch thick. Transfer it to a shallow 10-inch tart pan with a removable bottom and press to fit. Trim the edges even with the top of the pan, prick the bottom all over with a fork, and chill for 10 minutes to set.

Bake the tart for 25 to 30 minutes until golden brown, remove, and let cool on a cake rack.

To make the Berry Marmalade:

Gently stir the berries, sugar, and lemon juice together in a bowl and set aside.

To assemble the tart, spread a thin layer of berry jam on the bottom of the tart shell. Fill the entire tart with the lemon curd, using a metal spatula to make sure the top is completely smooth, then put it in the freezer for about 2 hours to set. Slide the sides from the pan and slice the tart into 8 even pieces. Serve each slice with a scoop of vanilla yogurt, spoon on some berry marmalade, and garnish with a couple of mint leaves.

Pasticcino di Cioccolato con Lampone Individual Chocolate Cakes with Fresh Raspberries

[MAKES 8 SERVINGS]

Chocolate lovers: these individually-sized intensely chocolatey cakes topped with cocoa-scented whipped cream and fresh raspberries are a simple but chocolate-satisfying dessert. Be aware, they are seductive!

Vegetable cooking spray

1⅓ cups cake flour, sifted

⅓ cup plus 2 tablespoons cocoa powder, sifted

Pinch of sea salt

¼ teaspoon baking soda

6 tablespoons unsalted butter

6 large eggs

1 cup granulated sugar

1 teaspoon vanilla extract

1 cup heavy cream

¼ cup confectioners' sugar, sifted

1 pint fresh raspberries

Preheat the oven to 325°F. Spray a standard muffin tin with nonstick spray or fill 8 of the cups with paper or foil liners.

Sift the flour, the ⅓ cup of cocoa, salt, and baking soda into a bowl and set aside. Melt the butter in a small saucepan and set aside.

Combine the eggs and sugar in the bowl of an electric mixer fitted with a whisk attachment. Set the bowl over a pan partially filled with simmering water. The water should not touch the bowl. Using a whisk, beat the egg-sugar mixture constantly until it feels very warm to the touch and all the sugar has dissolved. Immediately remove the bowl from the heat and transfer it to the electric mixer.

Whip the egg-sugar mixture on medium speed for 3 to 4 minutes until it triples in volume and is very thick and light colored. Add the vanilla and whip 2 to 3 seconds longer to blend. Remove the bowl from the mixer and gently fold in the flour-cocoa mixture.

Place about 1½ cups of the batter in a separate bowl and fold in the melted butter. Do this gently, as you do not want to overwork the batter. Fold this into the remaining batter. Divide the batter evenly among the cupcake tins. Bake in the center of the oven for 20 to 25 minutes, or until a toothpick or knife inserted in the center of one cupcake comes out clean. Remove and cool completely on a rack.

While the cupcakes are cooling, combine the heavy cream with the confectioners' sugar and the remaining 2 tablespoons of cocoa, beat into soft peaks, and set aside.

Remove the cupcakes from the tin and place them on dessert plates. Spoon the whipped cream on top, divide the raspberries among the plates, and serve.

Gelato alla Vaniglia Affogato in Caffè
Vanilla Ice Cream with Coffee Shots

This is my contemporary take on another traditional Italian dessert: gelato with hot espresso poured over it. I serve the pair in shot glasses. *Affogato* means choked or drowned, and when sweet gelato is drowned in strong coffee, the taste is reminiscent of a milkshake. The temperature contrast between the frozen gelato, hot espresso, and cool cream is great. You can double the recipe for larger portions and serve the dessert in bowls, if you prefer.

1 pint Vanilla Bean Gelato (page 240) or store-bought vanilla gelato

1 cup freshly brewed espresso

½ cup chilled heavy cream, whipped to soft peaks

In 8 small shot glasses, place 1 scoop (about ¼ cup each) of vanilla gelato. Fill the glasses with 2 tablespoons of espresso, top with the whipped cream, and place a small straw in each glass. Serve at once.

Tartine di Ciliege al Mascarpone
Individual Cherry Mascarpone Tartlets

[MAKES 6 SERVINGS]

Americans love Italian-style cheesecake with glazed cherries on top. This is our refined play on that theme: a delectable mascarpone, meringue, and whipped cream-filled tart topped with luscious cherries. What a way to go—especially in late spring when fresh cherries are in the market. At other times, use unsweetened frozen cherries.

Cornmeal Crust

5 tablespoons plus 1 teaspooon unsalted butter, softened

$\frac{1}{4}$ cup confectioners' sugar

1 large egg yolk

1 cup all-purpose flour, sifted

$\frac{1}{3}$ cup fine yellow or white cornmeal

Grated zest of 1 orange

$\frac{1}{4}$ teaspoon salt

Mascarpone Filling

$\frac{1}{2}$ cup mascarpone cheese

1 cup heavy cream

1 teaspoon vanilla extract

1 teaspoon powdered gelatin

2 large egg yolks

$\frac{1}{4}$ cup sugar

Topping

$1\frac{1}{2}$ cups pitted sour cherries or frozen unsweetened cherries,
    defrosted and drained

$\frac{1}{2}$ cup sugar

2 tablespoons cornstarch

Grated zest of 1 lemon, for garnish

¼ cup chopped pistachios, for garnish

To make the Cornmeal Crust:
In the bowl of a food processor, blend the butter and sugar together until smooth and fluffy.
Add the egg yolk and blend. Add the flour, cornmeal, orange zest, and salt and pulse until they
are just incorporated and the mixture resembles coarse meal; do not overmix. Remove the dough
from the bowl, gather into a ball, then flatten slightly into a disk, wrap in plastic wrap, and chill for
about 1 hour.

Preheat the oven to 325°F.

Unwrap the dough and divide it into six equal parts. On a lightly floured board, using a floured
rolling pin, roll the dough into circles about ¼-inch thick to fit into 3-inch tart pans. Trim the tops
even with the edges. Prick the bottoms all over. Bake the tarts for 10 to 12 minutes, until golden
brown. Remove from the oven and set aside on a rack to cool.

Meanwhile, to make the Mascarpone Filling:
Stir the mascarpone, ½ cup of the cream, and the vanilla in a bowl until smooth. Set aside.
Put 3 tablespoons of cold water in a small bowl. Sprinkle the gelatin over it and set aside to let it
absorb the liquid and soften.

In a large bowl, using an electric mixer with the whisk attachment, beat the egg yolks until
they have tripled in volume, at least 10 minutes. Combine the sugar and ¼ cup of water in a small
saucepan, bring to a rolling boil over high heat, and cook for 3 to 4 minutes until the sugar is
dissolved.

Remove the pan from the heat, beat in the softened gelatin, and pour the sugar syrup into the
yolks, beating until cool. Using a rubber spatula, fold the eggs into the mascarpone mixture. In a
mixing bowl, beat the remaining ½ cup of heavy cream into soft peaks and fold it into the filling.

To make the Topping:
Combine the cherries, sugar, and ¾ cup of water in a saucepan and bring to a boil. Dissolve the
cornstarch in enough water to make a smooth paste, then stir it into the cherries until smooth.
Boil until the sugar is dissolved and the liquid is clear, 2 to 3 minutes. Remove from the heat and
scrape the cherries into a metal bowl. Set the bowl into another bowl partially filled with ice to cool.

To assemble the tart, fill the tart shells to the rims with the mascarpone cream. (You may have a
little filling left over.) Refrigerate until set, about 1 hour. When firm, spoon the sour cherry compote
on top, garnish with lemon zest and chopped pistachios, and serve.

Torta di Mandorle e Albicocche alla Crema Almond Cake with Roasted Apricots and Vanilla Cream

This cake, with its nice almond flavor, has a tender crumb. It is elegantly dressed up with oven-roasted apricots with hints of honey, vanilla, and brandy.

Almond Cake

8 tablespoons (1 stick) unsalted butter, softened, plus butter to grease the pan

¾ cup sugar

½ cup almond paste, broken in small pieces

Grated zest of 1 orange

3 large eggs

½ cup all-purpose flour

¼ teaspoon baking powder

¼ teaspoon salt

1 cup sliced almonds

Roasted Apricots

10 firm ripe apricots, halved and pitted

2 vanilla beans, split lengthwise and seeds scraped

¼ cup honey

¼ cup apricot brandy

Vanilla Cream

1 cup heavy cream

¼ cup confectioners' sugar

Fresh thyme leaves, for garnish (see sidebar)

232

Preheat the oven to 325°F. Grease an 8-inch round cake pan with butter, line the bottom with parchment paper, and grease the parchment.

To make the almond cake:

Put the butter and sugar into the bowl of an electric mixer fitted with the paddle attachment. Add the almond paste and beat on low speed until smooth and fluffy, scraping down the sides of the bowl as necessary, 5 to 6 minutes. Add the orange zest, then add the eggs, one at a time and scraping after each addition, and beat until well blended (about 30 seconds each). Add the flour, baking powder, and salt and mix just until blended.

Using a rubber scraper, scrape the mixture into the prepared pan and smooth the top with a metal spatula. Sprinkle ½ cup of sliced almonds on top and bake in the middle of the oven for about 30 minutes, until the edges are golden brown and pulling away from the pan. Remove the pan from the oven, set it on a cake rack, and cool completely.

While the cake is baking, prepare the Roasted Apricots:

Put the apricots in a baking dish, and gently toss with one vanilla bean and its seeds and the honey. Pour in ¼ cup of water and the apricot brandy and toss again. Bake along with the cake, until the apricots are tender when pierced with the tip of a knife, 15 to 20 minutes; the timing will depend on the ripeness of the fruit.

To make the Vanilla Cream:

In a mixing bowl, whip the cream, confectioners' sugar, and seeds of the remaining vanilla bean into soft peaks.

To serve, lightly toast the remaining ¼ cup of almonds in a skillet over medium-low heat until golden and fragrant, 2 to 3 minutes. Invert the cake onto a cake plate and peel off the parchment. Turn the cake again so the almonds are on top. Cut the cake into 8 pieces and put on dessert plates. Top each slice with the roasted apricots, some of the liquid, and a spoonful of vanilla cream. Sprinkle with the toasted almonds and a few fresh thyme leaves and serve.

Using Herbs in Desserts

Tiny flowers, leaves, and sprigs of fresh herbs add a natural touch of color and a subtle, fresh taste to desserts. Just as a final sprinkle of chopped parsley dresses up savory dishes, uncooked herbs can do the same for sweets. For too long, pastry chefs plopped a strawberry on dessert plates to give them color, even when the berry had no connection with the flavors of the dish.

Adding an herb is more unexpected in sweets, but once you try it, I think you will agree that it imparts a unique, pleasurable dimension to the tastes. Look at the Vanilla Semifreddo with Pineapple Compote on page 203, where fresh tarragon has the same appropriate effect.

Crespelle di Nutella con Gelato alla Vaniglia e Nocciole

Nutella-Filled Crêpes with Vanilla Gelato and Salted Hazelnuts

[MAKES 8 SERVINGS]

These chocolate-filled crêpes with the most delicious candied and chocolate-enrobed hazelnuts are a mouth-watering finale to any meal. For speed and ease of preparation, you can buy delicious chocolate-coated nuts from peanuts to pistachios, as well as some excellent quality caramel sauce.

Chocolate-Covered Salted Hazelnuts

½ cup blanched whole hazelnuts

1 large egg white

1 tablespoon coarse salt

2 ounces bittersweet chocolate, chopped into small pieces

Caramel Sauce

1 cup sugar

1 teaspoon freshly squeezed lemon juice

⅔ cup heavy cream

½ tablespoon dark rum (optional)

1½ tablespoons unsalted butter

Crêpes

1¼ cups all-purpose flour

¼ cup sugar

1 teaspoon salt

6 large eggs

¾ cup milk

234

½ cup heavy cream

¼ cup dark rum

1 tablespoon vanilla extract

5 tablespoons unsalted butter, melted

1 cup Nutella

3 large ripe bananas, diced

1 quart Vanilla Bean Gelato (see page 240) or store-bought vanilla gelato

To make the Chocolate-Covered Salted Hazelnuts:

Preheat the toaster oven or oven to 325°F.

Spread the hazelnuts in a single layer in a shallow baking pan. Bake, shaking the pan occasionally, for 6 to 8 minutes until the nuts are lightly toasted. Turn the oven down to 300°F.

In a small bowl, stir the hazelnuts with the egg white to coat. Pour them into a strainer to let the excess egg white drain off. Put the nuts in a small plate, sprinkle on the salt, and toss to coat evenly. Transfer to a flat baking sheet and cook in the oven until golden brown, shaking the pan occasionally, 8 to 10 minutes. Remove and cool completely.

While the nuts are cooling, melt the chocolate in the top of a double boiler over simmering water, stirring until smooth, but don't let the insert touch the water. Remove the insert and let the chocolate cool to room temperature. Add the nuts to the melted chocolate and toss to coat. Transfer the nuts to a flat pan lined with waxed paper and set aside.

To make the Caramel Sauce:

In a small heavy saucepan, combine the sugar, ⅓ cup water, and lemon juice. Cook over low heat, stirring or swirling the pan often, until the sugar has completely dissolved. Raise the heat and boil gently, without stirring, until the sugar turns dark amber, about 5 minutes. Immediately remove from the heat and slowly whisk in the cream and rum, if using. Return the caramel to medium-low heat, whisk in the butter until smooth, and cook for 2 minutes longer. Remove the pan from the heat and set aside to let the caramel cool to room temperature.

To make the Crêpes:

In the bowl of a food processor, combine the flour, sugar, and salt and pulse a couple of times to blend. In a large measuring cup, beat the eggs, milk, cream, rum, and vanilla until blended. With the food processor motor running, slowly add the liquid ingredients through the feed tube until they are well incorporated, then add the butter, and process until blended. Pour the batter through a fine strainer into a bowl, cover, and chill for at least 30 minutes before using.

Heat an 8-inch nonstick skillet over medium heat. Ladle 2 tablespoons of the batter into the pan, swirling it to spread evenly. Cook until small brown spots form on the bottom of the crêpe, about 1 minute. Using a spatula or your fingers, flip the crêpe over and cook the second side until lightly browned, 15 to 20 seconds more. Flip the crêpe onto a flat tray. Repeat until all of the batter is used, placing pieces of waxed paper between each cooked crêpe. You should have 16 crêpes. Allow the crêpes to cool. You can also refrigerate them in a resealable plastic bag for a day or two.

To assemble and serve:

Spread each crêpe with about 1 tablespoon of Nutella and fold in quarters. Put 2 crêpes in the middle of each dessert plate. Mix the bananas with about ¼ cup of the caramel sauce and spoon them on the crêpes. Sprinkle on the chocolate hazelnuts and add a couple of small scoops of gelato on either side of the crêpes. Drizzle on the remaining caramel sauce and serve at once.

Coppa di Tiramisù
Tiramisù Cup

[MAKES 8 SERVINGS]

Are you bored with traditional-style tiramisù? This updated interpretation includes layers of chocolate, espresso, and mascarpone attractively served in a glass. Serve the dessert with store-bought ladyfinger cookies on the side.

Chocolate Cream

    1 teaspoon powdered gelatin

    2 ounces milk chocolate, finely chopped

    2 ounces bittersweet chocolate, finely chopped

    1½ cups heavy cream

    ¼ cup sugar

Espresso Cream

    1 teaspoon powdered gelatin

    2 ounces bittersweet chocolate, finely chopped

    ¼ cup instant espresso powder, plus extra for sprinkling

    1½ cups heavy cream

    ¼ cup sugar

Mascarpone Cream

    ½ cup mascarpone

    ¼ cup confectioners' sugar

    ¼ cup heavy cream

To make the Chocolate Cream:

In a small bowl, sprinkle the gelatin over 2 tablespoons of cold water and set it aside to absorb the liquid and soften.

Place the milk chocolate and bittersweet chocolate in a medium-size bowl. Combine the heavy cream and sugar in a small saucepan and bring to a boil over medium heat. Remove the pan from the heat and whisk in the gelatin until dissolved. Pour the cream mixture over the chopped chocolates and whisk together until smooth and blended. Spoon the mixture evenly into the bottom of 8 tall dessert glasses. Place in the refrigerator to set for about 1 hour.

To make the Espresso Cream:

In a small bowl, sprinkle the gelatin over 2 tablespoons cold water and set it aside to absorb the liquid.

Combine the chocolate and espresso powder in a small bowl. Combine the heavy cream and sugar in a small saucepan and bring to a boil over medium heat. Remove the pan from the heat and whisk in the gelatin to dissolve. Pour the cream mixture over the chocolate and espresso and whisk until combined.

Remove the dessert glasses with the chocolate cream from the refrigerator. Spoon the espresso cream evenly on top of the chocolate cream and return the glasses to the refrigerator to chill for about 1 hour.

Meanwhile, to make the Mascarpone Cream:

Remove the mascarpone from the refrigerator and let it come to room temperature, about 1 hour. Put it in a small bowl and, using a rubber spatula, fold in the confectioners' sugar. Fold in the heavy cream and refrigerate until ready to serve.

To serve, remove the dessert glasses from the refrigerator and place a spoonful of the mascarpone cream on top of the espresso cream. Sprinkle the mascarpone cream with a little instant espresso powder and serve.

Gelato alla Vaniglia
Vanilla Bean Gelato

[MAKES 1 QUART]

The word gelato simply means "frozen" in Italian. For the uninitiated, that word can't convey how smooth and rich this creamy dessert is. While gelato bears a passing resemblance to American ice cream, it is whipped with less air, which gives it a denser texture.

Gelati are made with about three parts milk to one part cream, rather than all cream, as are its American cousins. With less butterfat to coat the tongue, the flavors really shine through. In this version, for example, you really taste the lush vanilla bean.

While there are very sophisticated gelato-making machines on the market, home model ice cream machines do a fine job. As variations to this basic recipe, you might add chopped fruits, candy, or nuts to the ice cream maker when the custard is a minute or two from being frozen.

3 cups milk

1 cup heavy cream

1 cup sugar

3 vanilla beans, split lengthwise and seeds scraped, or 3 tablespoons vanilla extract

3 large egg yolks

Combine the milk, cream, and sugar in a medium-size nonreactive saucepan. Add the vanilla beans and seeds to the mixture, or add the vanilla extract. Bring the mixture to a boil over medium heat, stirring from time to time, until the sugar is dissolved, about 10 minutes.

Meanwhile, beat the egg yolks in a small bowl. Slowly whisk ½ cup of the hot milk-cream mixture into the yolks, then return the warmed yolks to the milk-cream mixture, stirring continuously. Reduce the heat to medium-low and cook, stirring constantly, for about 20 minutes, until the mixture is thick enough to coat the back of a wooden spoon or measures 190°F on an instant-read thermometer. Remove the

240

pan from the heat and pour the mixture through a fine strainer into a metal bowl. Put the bowl in another bowl partially filled with ice and stir to chill completely. Transfer the liquid to the canister of an ice cream maker and freeze according to the manufacturer's instructions for gelato. When frozen, transfer the gelato to an airtight container and store in the freezer.

Vanilla Beans and Vanilla Extract

Vanilla beans are available in many supermarkets in little glass vials or plastic bags. Compared with the extract, they offer a pure, floral taste of vanilla. Even the experience of working with them is sensual, since once you cut and scrape the beans, your fingers retain that lovely smell two hours later.

Use a sharp paring knife and split the bean lengthwise, then scrape away the seeds. In our recipes, often both the bean and seeds are used in cooking since a lot of the seeds get left in the bean.

To substitute extract for a vanilla bean, use about 1 tablespoon per bean.

Gelato al Miele Millefiori
Wildflower Honey Gelato

[MAKES 1 QUART]

Intensely floral-tasting honey imparts a lovely note to this gelato.

1 cup wildflower honey or substitute any other honey

3 cups whole milk

1 cup heavy cream

8 large egg yolks

Pour the honey into a small saucepan and bring to a boil. Cook until it thickens slightly, 3 to 4 minutes, then stir in the milk and cream and return the liquid to a boil, stirring often. Remove the pan from the heat. In a small bowl, beat the egg yolks until smooth. Stir about ½ cup of the hot milk-cream mixture into the egg yolks, then return the warmed yolks to the milk-cream mixture. Return the pan to the heat and cook over medium-low heat, stirring constantly, until the mixture is thick enough to coat the back of a wooden spoon or measures 190°F on an instant-read thermometer.

Remove the pan from the heat and pour the mixture through a fine strainer into a metal bowl. Put the bowl in another bowl partially filled with ice and stir to chill completely. Transfer the liquid to the canister of an ice cream maker and freeze according to the manufacturer's instructions for gelato. When frozen, transfer the gelato to an airtight container and store in the freezer.

Gelato alle More
Blackberry Gelato

[MAKES 1 QUART]

Combine fresh cream and juicy, seasonal blackberries (or frozen ones) and you get this irresistible gelato. Fresh berries can be quite tart, so taste them before adding. You may want to add a little more sugar. If using frozen berries, buy those that are unsweetened.

3 cups milk

1 cup heavy cream

1 cup sugar

3 large egg yolks

3 cups fresh or frozen blackberries

Combine the milk, cream, and sugar in a medium-size nonreactive saucepan. Bring the mixture to a boil over medium heat, stirring from time to time, until the sugar is dissolved, about 10 minutes.

While the cream is cooking, beat the egg yolks in a small bowl. Slowly whisk ½ cup of the hot milk-cream mixture into the yolks, then return the warmed yolks to the milk-cream mixture, stirring continuously. Reduce the heat to medium-low and cook, stirring constantly, until the mixture is thick enough to coat the back of a wooden spoon or measures 190°F on an instant-read thermometer.

Remove the pan from the heat and pour the mixture through a fine strainer into a metal bowl. Put the bowl in another bowl partially filled with ice and stir to chill completely. Meanwhile, purée the blackberries in a food processor. Pour through a strainer, pressing with a rubber spatula to extract as much liquid as possible. When the custard is cold, stir in the blackberries.

Transfer the liquid to the canister of an ice cream maker and freeze according to the manufacturer's instructions for gelato. When frozen, transfer the gelato to an airtight container and store in the freezer.

Moca Gelato
Mocha Gelato

[MAKES 1 QUART]

People love chocolate and people love espresso. Combining them in creamy gelato is a heavenly partnership; it is one of Fiamma's most popular flavors. For optimal flavor, grind fresh espresso beans into a fine powder.

3 cups milk

1 cup heavy cream

1 cup sugar

½ cup finely ground espresso coffee beans

3 large egg yolks

1 cup finely chopped bittersweet chocolate

Combine the milk, cream, sugar, and espresso in a medium-size nonreactive saucepan. Bring the mixture to a boil over medium heat, stirring from time to time, until the sugar is dissolved, about 10 minutes.

While the milk is cooking, beat the egg yolks in a small bowl. Slowly whisk ½ cup of the hot milk-cream mixture into the yolks, then return the warmed yolks to the milk-cream mixture, stirring continuously. Reduce the heat to medium-low and cook, stirring constantly, until the mixture is thick enough to coat the back of a wooden spoon or measures 190°F on an instant-read thermometer. Remove the pan from the heat and pour the mixture through a fine strainer into a metal bowl. Add the chocolate and stir until it is completely melted.

Put the bowl in another bowl partially filled with ice and stir to chill completely. Transfer the liquid to the canister of an ice cream maker and freeze according to the manufacturer's instructions for gelato. When frozen, transfer the gelato to an airtight container and store in the freezer.

Gelato di Yogurt alla Vaniglia
Vanilla Frozen Yogurt

Frozen yogurt made with whole milk yogurt and real vanilla is a revelation compared with what you buy in the local supermarket.

½ cup sugar

2 cups plain whole milk or low-fat yogurt

1 vanilla bean, split lengthwise and seeds scraped,
or 1 tablespoon vanilla extract

In a small saucepan, bring 1 cup water and the sugar to a rolling boil and cook for 3 to 4 minutes. Remove the pan from the heat and cool completely, about 20 minutes.

In a bowl, whisk the yogurt and vanilla seeds together until smooth. Whisk in the sugar syrup until blended. Transfer the mixture to the canister of an ice cream maker and freeze according to the manufacturer's instructions for gelato. When frozen, serve at once, or transfer to an airtight container and freeze.

Trio di Sorbetti
Sorbet Trio

[EACH RECIPE MAKES 1 QUART]

S orbetti are made with lightly sweetened, unstrained fruit purées. These smooth, almost creamy desserts are welcome all year but especially during those blistering hot days and nights of summer. They rely on the freshest fruit in the marketplace. *Sorbetti* are simply puréed, often with the skin left on, to retain their texture.

Sorbetto di Rabarbaro
Rhubarb Sorbet

4 cups trimmed and diced fresh rhubarb (20 small or 15 medium stalks)

¾ cup sugar

2 tablespoons freshly squeezed lemon juice

1 vanilla bean, split lengthwise and seeds scraped

Place the rhubarb, 2 cups water, sugar, lemon juice, and vanilla bean and seeds in a medium-size saucepan and bring to a boil over medium-high heat, stirring from time to time to dissolve the sugar. Reduce the heat to medium and simmer, stirring occasionally, for 10 minutes.

Remove the pan from the heat and remove the vanilla bean. Blend the mixture into a purée with an immersion blender or transfer it to an electric blender and blend in small batches on low speed until smooth. Pour the *sorbetto* into a metal bowl, place it inside another bowl partially filled with ice, and stir until it is chilled completely. Transfer the *sorbetto* to the canister of an ice cream maker and freeze according to the manufacturer's directions. Freeze in an airtight container.

Sorbetto di Mango
Mango Sorbet

6 to 8 ripe mangoes (to make 4 cups)

1 cup sugar

To get the most flesh from each mango, figure out which is the flat side of the mango; that is the wide side of the large seed inside. Slice off a tiny sliver from one end of each mango on which to stand it up. Stand it on the base and cut off the side of the mango as close to the seed as possible. Turn and cut off the other side along the seed. You will still have the skin on the mango and a small horizontal strip of unpeeled flesh on both sides next to the pit. Using a spoon, scoop out the flesh from each piece and cut it into small cubes. You should have about 4 cups of mango.

Combine the mango, 2 cups water, and sugar in a medium-size saucepan and bring to a boil over medium-high heat, stirring from time to time to dissolve the sugar. Reduce the heat to medium and simmer, stirring occasionally, for 5 minutes. Pour the *sorbetto* into a metal bowl, place the bowl in another bowl partially filled with ice, and stir until it is chilled completely. Transfer the *sorbetto* to the canister of an ice cream maker and freeze according to the manufacturer's directions. Freeze in an airtight container.

Sorbetto di Mele Verdi
Green Apple Sorbet

1 cup sugar

4 cups cored and diced green apple with the skin on (3 to 4 medium apples)

Combine 2 cups water and the sugar in a small saucepan, bring to a boil, and cook without stirring until the sugar is completely dissolved, 2 to 3 minutes. Remove the pan from the heat and chill for 20 minutes.

In a bowl, combine the sugar syrup with the chopped raw apples. Blend with an immersion blender or transfer to an electric blender and purée until smooth. Transfer the *sorbetto* to the canister of an ice cream maker and freeze according to the manufacturer's directions. Freeze in an airtight container.

ricette di base

Sale Speziato Rosemary Salt Olio d'Oliva al Limone Lemon Olive Oil Brodo di Pesce Fish Stock Brodo di Pollo Homemade Chicken Stock Fondo di Pollo Rich Chicken Stock Brodo di Vitello Veal Stock Sugo di Pomodoro Basic Tomato Sauce Salsa Verde Green Sauce Maionese di Funghi Wild Mushroom Mayonnaise Mostarda alla Cremona Cremona-Style Mostarda Burro al Tartufo Truffle Butter

STAPLES

All of the great cooks

I know rely on certain staples to add their own unique signature to food. It begins with homemade stocks and sauces as the foundation for a dish. Favorite seasonings and condiments are also used during the preparation and, in some cases, as the final ingredient before a dish is served. Although they may seem like insignificant additions, these sauces, condiments, and seasonings all have the power to transform a simple dish into one that is a standout.

In my kitchen, Rosemary Salt (page 253) and Lemon Olive Oil (page 253) are two essentials. I list them at the beginning of this chapter because I use them both so often. You will notice Rosemary Salt is called for as a seasoning for fish, poultry, and meat in this book, and I finish everything from salads and pasta dishes to vegetables and main courses with a few drops of lemon-infused olive oil. Once you experience how they can enhance many dishes, you will probably reach for one or both even when I don't suggest them.

The merits of cooking with homemade stocks have been described by countless chefs in numerous books. I, too, want to emphasize their importance when you aspire to cook exceptional-tasting foods. The differences between the Fish Stock (page 254) and Rich Chicken Stock (page 256) made from scratch in this chapter and those you can buy are especially dramatic.

When it comes to sauces and condiments, I have included a few of my "must haves" to add to your repertoire. If you want to transform boiled pasta or grilled chicken into something extraordinary, add a little Truffle Butter (page 264). Those plain foods—and many others— will take on a luxurious aspect as your mouth is flooded with the woodsy tuber's musky, nutty taste in the creamy butter.

Basic mayonnaise becomes unique when blended with wild mushrooms. It is superb on roast pork sandwiches. Green Sauce (page 261) is another simple sauce to use with cold roasted meats, fish, and poultry. Even my Basic Tomato Sauce (page 260), so easy to make, is surprisingly better than most jarred varieties you can buy.

Finally, Mostarda is a condiment that only recently has become available in America. I simply adore this sweet-mustardy condiment from Cremona served with Bollito Misto (page 175), where it is almost required. It is also delicious with roast chicken, or with a tiny dollop of the condiment spooned on cubes of creamy cheese, to name but a few places to use it.

Sale Speziato
Rosemary Salt

[MAKES 1½ CUPS] Abasic seasoning for poultry, meat, and fish. Add it to salads and vegetables, as well. Stored in an airtight container in the refrigerator, it will last for at least a month.

1 cup coarse sea salt

½ cup fresh rosemary leaves or 3 tablespoons dried rosemary leaves

¼ cup fresh sage leaves or 1½ tablespoons dried sage leaves

3 cloves garlic, split lengthwise in half

3 tablespoons black peppercorns

Freshly grated zest of 1 lemon

Combine the salt, rosemary, sage, garlic, peppercorns, and lemon zest in a food processor and pulse until fairly finely ground and the lemon's natural oils have been evenly distributed. Transfer to a container and refrigerate.

Olio d'Oliva al Limone
Lemon Olive Oil

[MAKES 1 QUART] This citrus-scented oil is simple to make, yet once you have it on your shelf, you will find countless uses for it. Use it as a final drizzle on salads, grilled or broiled fish and chicken, and over sautéed vegetables.

5 lemons

1 quart mild-flavored extra-virgin olive oil

Wash the skins of the lemons to remove all wax and dirt. Dry thoroughly. Using a sharp paring knife or vegetable peeler, remove the colored zest in strips. Reserve the lemons for another use. Add the zest to the olive oil, close the bottle, and set it in a windowsill for up to a week to infuse, then refrigerate for up to a month. Remove and return to room temperature before using.

Brodo di Pesce
Fish Stock

[MAKES ABOUT 2 QUARTS]

This recipe is emphatically superior to purchased fish stocks and bottled clam juice. The stock should have a clean, fresh fish taste without excess saltiness. Markets with service seafood counters and fish markets regularly fillet non-oily, white fish, such as cod, striped bass, and sole. With a little notice, they will generally give you the bones and trimmings. Store the stock in the refrigerator for 3 to 4 days or freeze it for up to 3 months in an airtight container.

2 cups dry white wine, such as Pinot Grigio

⅓ cup white wine vinegar

2 whole medium yellow onions, each stuck with 3 whole cloves

2 medium carrots, peeled and coarsely chopped

1 large rib celery with leaves, trimmed and coarsely chopped

3 sprigs fresh flat-leaf parsley

1 sprig fresh thyme

1 bay leaf

½ tablespoon salt

Trimmings and bones from 2 to 3 lean white, non-oily fish

Combine 1½ quarts water, the wine, vinegar, onions, carrots, celery, parsley, thyme, bay leaf, and salt in a large pot and bring to a boil. Add the fish trimmings and bones, turn the heat down so the liquid is simmering, cover, and cook for 1 hour.

Strain the stock through several layers of cheesecloth into a clean pan. Taste to adjust the seasonings and reduce the stock over high heat, if needed, to intensify the flavor. Store in a clean, airtight container in the refrigerator or freezer.

Brodo di Pollo
Homemade Chicken Stock

[MAKES ABOUT 2 QUARTS]

This makes a lot of chicken stock. You can cut the recipe in half, but if you use chicken stock as often as I do, it's just as easy to make a large quantity as a small amount, then freeze it for future use.

10 pounds chicken carcasses or wings, backs, and ribs, chopped into 1½-inch pieces (see Note)

3 large carrots, coarsely chopped

3 large unpeeled yellow onions, quartered

2 large ribs celery including leaves, coarsely chopped

6 large sprigs flat-leaf parsley

10 black peppercorns

3 bay leaves

1 tablespoon salt

1½ gallons water

Combine the chicken, carrots, onions, celery, parsley, peppercorns, bay leaves, and salt in a large deep stockpot. Add enough water to cover the chicken, about 1½ gallons. Bring the water to just below the boiling point over high heat, then reduce the heat so the liquid is gently simmering. Partially cover and cook for 2 to 2½ hours, skimming off any scum that rises to the surface, then let cool.

When cool, strain the stock through cheesecloth. Do not press on the solids or the stock will become cloudy. Discard the bones, herbs, and vegetables. Cover and refrigerate for up to 3 days, or freeze for 5 to 6 months. Skim off the congealed surface fat before using.

Note: Get in the habit of saving chicken parts, such as the wings, backs, and ribs, each time you cut up a chicken. Some markets sell these for a nominal amount. Put them into a resealable plastic bag or container and store in the freezer until you have a sufficient amount to make stock.

Fondo di Pollo
Rich Chicken Stock

[MAKES ABOUT 4 QUARTS]

Chicken bones and aromatic vegetables are first browned before water and wine are added to the pot for this rich-tasting stock. I think you will be surprised at how it enhances the flavor of a dish. The stock will last for three to four days in the refrigerator or for six months in the freezer when stored in an airtight container.

2 tablespoons olive oil

3 pounds uncooked chicken carcasses with a little meat on them, plus wings, backs, and ribs chopped into 1½-inch pieces

1 medium-large yellow onion, chopped (1 cup)

2 medium ribs celery with leaves, trimmed and chopped (¾ cup)

1 medium carrot, peeled and chopped (¾ cup)

5 cloves garlic, cut in half

1 tomato, chopped

1 tablespoon tomato paste

½ cup dry white wine, such as Pinot Grigio or Trebbiano

2 bay leaves

5 sprigs fresh flat-leaf parsley

4 sprigs fresh thyme

Sea salt and freshly ground black pepper

Heat the olive oil in a large deep skillet or roasting pan over medium-high heat until hot. Add the chicken bones and cook until golden brown, 8 to 10 minutes, turning occasionally. Add the onion, celery, carrot, and garlic and cook, stirring occasionally, until the vegetables are golden brown, 7 to 8 minutes.

Stir in the tomato and tomato paste and cook, stirring occasionally, for 5 minutes. Pour in the white wine and cook for 2 minutes more. Add 2 quarts water, bay leaves, parsley, and thyme. Simmer for 1 hour, skimming the surface from time to time. Pour the liquid through a fine strainer into a clean pot, pressing to extract as much liquid as possible. Season to taste with salt and pepper. To intensify the flavor, if desired, reduce the stock over high heat. The stock will last for 3 to 4 days in the refrigerator or for 6 months in the freezer when stored in an airtight container.

Brodo di Vitello
Veal Stock

[MAKES 2 QUARTS]

This flavorful veal stock is the basis
for wonderful soups, stews, and sauces. If reduced by half, it becomes demi-glace.
Reduced to a thick, gelatinous consistency—about a quarter of its original volume—
it's known as *glace de viande,* or meat glaze. At that point, the flavor is very intense.
A little of this "amber gold" added to any dish will dramatically enrich the flavor.
The stock keeps for three days in the refrigerator or for five to six months frozen.
Most markets sell bones that are already cut into 2-inch lengths and, when large,
already cracked. If not, ask your butcher to do this for you.

8 pounds meaty raw veal bones (or veal and beef bones),
   cracked if large, and cut into 2-inch lengths

3 medium carrots, peeled and cut in 2-inch lengths

2 large unpeeled yellow onions, split with 1 clove stuck in each half

1 leek or the green tops of 2 leeks, trimmed, rinsed, and split in half lengthwise

1 large rib celery with leaves, trimmed and cut into 2-inch lengths

One 28-ounce can plum tomatoes, undrained

3 sprigs fresh flat-leaf parsley

2 sprigs fresh thyme or 1 teaspoon dried thyme

4 large unpeeled cloves garlic, split

5 black peppercorns

½ teaspoon salt, optional (see Note)

Preheat the oven to 400°F.

Put the bones in a large shallow roasting pan and roast until richly browned on all sides, turning
occasionally, about 1 hour. Pour off almost all the fat. Add the carrots, onions (cut side down), leek,

258

and celery to the pan and roast until the vegetables have started to brown and caramelize, about 15 minutes longer.

Transfer the bones and vegetables to a large stockpot and set the roasting pan aside. Add 8 to 10 quarts cold water to the stockpot and bring just to a boil. Adjust the heat down so the liquid is simmering. Skim off any scum that rises to the surface during the first hour.

Meanwhile, deglaze the roasting pan with 1 cup warm water, scraping up all the browned bits with a wooden spoon, and add this liquid to the stockpot. Stir in the tomatoes, parsley, thyme, garlic, peppercorns, and salt, if using. Partially cover and simmer for at least 4 hours, adding water if needed to cover the ingredients by at least 2 inches.

Strain the stock into a clean pot, pressing to extract as much liquid as possible. Return to a slow boil and cook until the liquid is reduced to 2 quarts. Transfer to a large bowl, cover, and refrigerate overnight. Skim off the layer of fat on the surface and discard. The stock may be refrigerated or frozen until needed.

Alternatively, return the stock to the pot, bring to a boil, and boil rapidly to reduce it to a demi-glace or *glace de viande*. As the stock thickens, adjust the heat to low and watch to make sure it doesn't burn. Refrigerated *glace de viande* lasts for several days. Cut into cubes and frozen in small resealable plastic bags, it keeps for 5 to 6 months. You may also pour it into ice cube trays, cover tightly, and use the cubes as you need them.

Note: The vegetables and meat have a certain amount of natural salt. If you plan to make *glace de viande,* no additional salt is needed.

Sugo di Pomodoro
Basic Tomato Sauce

[MAKES 2 QUARTS]

This quick and easy tomato sauce can be prepared and served immediately or refrigerated in a tightly covered container for up to five days. It freezes well in airtight containers, as well. Make sure to leave some headroom for expansion. High quality canned plum tomatoes are generally superior to fresh tomatoes for sauces and stews except in the summer when regional, vine-ripened varieties are available.

3 tablespoons olive oil

1 large yellow onion, chopped (1¼ cups)

2 large cloves garlic, crushed

One 28-ounce can crushed Italian tomatoes, undrained

3 tablespoons chopped fresh basil

Sea salt and freshly ground black pepper

In a large, heavy nonreactive saucepan, heat the oil over medium-high heat until hot and fragrant. Stir in the onion and cook, stirring, until soft but not brown, 5 to 6 minutes. Stir in the garlic and cook for about 30 seconds longer. Stir in the tomatoes, basil, salt, and pepper. Simmer, partially covered, over medium-low heat for at least 30 to 40 minutes, stirring occasionally with a wooden spoon. Taste to adjust the seasonings before serving.

Salsa Verde
Green Sauce

[MAKES 1¼ CUPS]

This highly aromatic green sauce can be served with *Bollito Misto* (page 175), grilled chicken, or any place you want a tasty fresh salsa.

¾ cup extra-virgin olive oil

½ cup loosely packed chopped fresh flat-leaf parsley

½ cup loosely packed chopped fresh mint leaves

⅓ cup chopped scallions, including most of the green part

¼ cup capers, drained and coarsely chopped

2 oil-packed anchovy fillets, rinsed and patted dry with paper towels

Sea salt and freshly ground black pepper

Freshly squeezed lemon juice

Combine the olive oil, parsley, mint, scallions, capers, and anchovies in the jar of an electric blender and blend until smooth. Season to taste with salt, pepper, and lemon juice. Serve at once or transfer the sauce to a glass jar with a tight-fitting lid and reserve in the refrigerator for up to 2 days.

Maionese di Funghi
Wild Mushroom Mayonnaise

[MAKES ABOUT 1½ CUPS]

This delicious condiment is just what a plain cold roast chicken, grilled salmon, or swordfish needs to dress it up. Or spread it on a sandwich. Besides reconstituted porcini you could use other dried wild mushrooms as well as any variety of sliced fresh mushrooms sautéed in olive oil with some minced shallots, chopped parsley, and thyme added. (In which case, cook about 1½ cups of mushrooms). I use a mixture of olive and canola oil to make the mayonnaise less dense. Store the mayonnaise in a tightly covered container in the refrigerator for up to a week.

1 ounce dried porcini or other wild mushrooms

2 large egg yolks, at room temperature

1½ tablespoons freshly squeezed lemon juice or vinegar

1 small clove garlic, minced

¼ teaspoon sea salt

½ cup fruity extra-virgin olive oil

¾ cup canola oil

Cayenne pepper

Combine the porcini and enough warm water to cover in a small bowl and let them soak until the mushrooms are softened, 15 to 20 minutes. Strain through a sieve lined with cheesecloth or a double layer of paper towels. Reserve the soaking liquid. Pat the mushrooms dry with paper towels. Remove any grit, finely chop, and set aside.

Combine the egg yolks, lemon juice or vinegar, garlic, and salt in a large bowl. Beat with a whisk until pale and frothy, about 30 seconds. Slowly whisk in the olive oil, drizzling it into the yolk mixture a little bit at a time, until the mayonnaise is emulsified and thickened. Repeat the process with the canola oil. If the mayonnaise is too thick, thin it out by whisking in some of the reserved mushroom liquid, 1 tablespoon at a time. Stir in the mushrooms, season to taste with salt and cayenne, and serve.

Mostarda alla Cremona
Cremona-Style Mostarda

[MAKES ABOUT 8 CUPS]

This is my version of *mostarda*,
a sweet- and sour-tasting condiment made with fruit preserved in syrup.
Powdered mustard adds its characteristic kick. It is one of the standard sauces served with
Bollito Misto (page 175), and it varies in texture from chunky to almost smooth with just bits
of visible fruit. A spoonful or two is sometimes added to the filling of Pasta Hats Filled
with Butternut Squash, Amaretti, and Parmigiano-Reggiano with Sage Butter Sauce (page 81).
Although mostarda is found throughout northern Italy, the best known version
is from Cremona, where it is sold in many shops. Some are thicker, like marmalade.
Others are looser, like mine. A jar of this condiment is a nice gift to offer to friends who invite you
for dinner. When properly sealed in glass jars, it will last for several months in a cool spot.
Otherwise, it will keep for at least four months when refrigerated in a screw-top jar.

2½ cups sugar

2 ripe quinces or green apples, peeled, cored, and cut into ¼-inch slices

3 firm ripe pears, such as Anjou, peeled, cored, and cut into ¼-inch slices

½ pound apricots, peeled, pitted, and coarsely chopped

½ pound peaches, peeled, pitted, and coarsely chopped

½ pound figs, washed and stems removed, or substitute
   dried figs plumped for 30 minutes in water

⅓ pound dark cherries, washed and pitted

2 cups white wine vinegar

3 to 4 tablespoons powdered mustard, according to taste

Bring 4 cups water to a simmer in a large nonreactive pot. Slowly stir in the sugar. When it has
dissolved, add the quinces or apples and cook gently for 15 minutes. Stir in the pears, apricots, and

peaches, cook for 5 minutes, then add the figs and cherries and cook gently for 10 minutes more. Remove the pot from the heat and set aside to cool.

Meanwhile, combine the vinegar and mustard in a small saucepan and bring to a boil. Remove from the heat and cool. Drain the syrup from the fruits into the mustard mixture and bring back to a boil. Cook until it is reduced by half, about 20 minutes. It will thicken slightly as it cools. Pour the syrup over the fruits, stir to mix, then transfer the *mostarda* to jars and seal tightly. Store in a cool, dark spot.

Burro al Tartufo
Truffle Butter

[MAKES ⅓ CUP]

Use this delectable butter on pasta, baked or boiled potatoes, chicken, and salmon steaks. Those are only a few of the numerous places where it would greatly enhance a meal. Store it in a tightly covered container in the refrigerator for up to a week.

8 tablespoons (1 stick) unsalted butter, softened

1 ounce black truffle paste (see Sources, page 266)

1 ounce black truffle oil (see Sources, page 266)

Pinch of sea salt

In a small bowl, stir the butter, truffle paste, and truffle oil together into a smooth mixture. Season to taste with sea salt, then set aside at room temperature for about 2 hours for the flavors to blend before using.

Sources

· ·

AGATA & VALENTINA
1505 First Avenue
New York, New York 10021
212-452-0690
Superb Italian grocery on Manhattan's Upper East Side with many hard-to-find cheeses, Italian sausages, fish, and breads.

AIDELLS SAUSAGE COMPANY
1625 Alvarado Street
San Leandro, California 94577
877-AIDELLS
www.aidells.com
Sausage king Bruce Aidells has many varieties of sausages and plenty of wisdom to share on all related matters.

ALLEVA BROTHERS
188 Grand Street
New York, New York 10013
800-4 ALLEVA (800-425-5382)
www.allevadairy.com
Fresh ricotta, fresh and dried sausages, pasta and ravioli, as well as Sicilian cheeses and breads.

BALDUCCI'S
Locations in New York, Connecticut, Maryland, Virginia, and District of Columbia

800-346-8763
www.balduccis.com
Great effort has been made to revitalize this once trailblazing store. Ramped-up salumeria, imported and artisanal oils, vinegars, pastas, grains, truffles, and superb cheeses.

BIANCARDI'S
2350 Arthur Avenue
Bronx, New York 10458
718-733-4058
The celebrated butcher shop in the Bronx, on Arthur Avenue, where chefs and locals shop for superb meats to order, homemade fresh and dried sausages, prosciutto, Parmigiano-Reggiano, etc. With a little notice, they will special order many delicacies.

BUONITALIA
75 Ninth Avenue
New York, New York 10011
212-633-9090
www.buonitalia.com
Located in Chelsea Market, New York, they offer an authentic array of imported artisanal pasta, grains, truffles, and cheese.

CHEF'S WAREHOUSE/BEL CANTO FANCY FOODS LIMITED
1300 Viele Avenue
Bronx, New York 10474
800-878-3247
718-497-3888
www.chefswarehouse.com
Website purchases only. Fresh black and white truffles, truffle and olive oil, imported rice, *saba*, and aged balsamic vinegar.

CORTI BROTHERS
5810 Folsom Boulevard
Sacramento, California 75819
800-509-3663
www.cortibros.biz
Renowned in California and across the country for decades, this emporium sells many unique and rare Italian items including Tuscan beans, truffles, premium balsamic vinegars, and fine oils.

D'ARTAGNAN
120 Wilson Avenue
Newark, New Jersey 07105
800-DARTAGNAN
www.dartagnan.com
The paramount source for game birds and meats, foie gras, wild mushrooms, truffles, truffle butter, and oils.

DEAN & DELUCA
75 University Place, 560 Broadway, and
2 Rockefeller Center
New York, New York
800-999-0306
www.deandeluca.com
Top-flight international specialty food source for cheeses, herbs and spices, specialty rices, dried fruits and nuts, pastas, oils, and vinegars.

DIPALO DAIRY
206 Grand Street
New York, New York 10013
212-226-1033
Decades-old shop in Little Italy produces excellent mozzarella and imports exceptional Italian regional cheeses and charcuterie, as well as oils and vinegars. Although always busy, the friendly staff will happily discuss the finer points of a *piave* or *scamorza*.

DOMINGO'S ITALIAN GROCERY
17548 Ventura Boulevard
Encino, California 91316
818-981-4466
Broad selection of Italian cheeses and sausages, olives, fresh pastas, and condiments.

FAIRWAY
2328 Twelfth Avenue and 2127 Broadway
New York, New York
212-234-3883
212-595-1888
www.fairwaymarket.com
Freshest produce, cheese, meats, seafood, pasta, and oils.

FOX & OBEL
401 East Illinois Street
Chicago, Illinois 60611
312-410-7301
www.fox-obel.com
A modern service-oriented market with some harder-to-find Italian products like *speck*, imported prosciutto, truffles and truffle oil, fresh artichoke hearts, pastas, and sausages.

GEPPERTH'S MEAT MARKET
1964 North Halsted Street
Chicago, Illinois 60614
773-549-3883
www.gepperthsmarket.com
A congenial atmosphere pervades this nearly 100-year-old butcher shop that sells exceptional veal, poultry, and housemade sausages.

GUIDO'S FRESH MARKETPLACE
760 Main Street
Great Barrington, Massachusetts 01230
413-528-9255
www.guidosfreshmarketplace.com
A magnet for vacationers and area residents for the exceptional imported and locally made pastas, sausages, Italian cheeses, oils, breads, fish, olive oil, and fresh and dried wild mushrooms.

IDEAL CHEESE SHOP
942 First Avenue
New York, New York 10022
800-382-0109
www.idealcheese.com
Since 1954, this Upper East Side New York shop has introduced dozens of exotic cheeses to the American marketplace. They also sell imported oils, vinegars, butter, and mustard.

LITTERI'S
517-519 Morse Street, N.E.
Washington, D.C. 20002
202-544-0184
www.litteris.com
A favorite destination among locals since 1926 for Italian pastas, cheese, sausages, condiments, and wines.

MANGANARO'S
488 Ninth Avenue
New York, New York 10018
800-4SALAMI
www.manganaros.com
This midtown Manahattan grocery has sold fresh and dried sausages, Sicilian olive oils, imported Italian tuna and anchovies, and fresh and dried pastas for over 100 years.

P. G. MOLINARI AND SONS
1401 Yosemite Avenue
San Francisco, California 94124
415-822-5555
www.molinarisalame.com
Smoked and cured Italian salami and sausages since 1896.

THE MOZZARELLA COMPANY
2944 Elm Street
Dallas, Texas 75226
800-798-2954
www.mozzco.com
Paula Lambert and her staff have been making and shipping a wide range of fresh Italian sheep and cow's milk cheeses since 1982.

Sources

....

THE PASTA SHOP AT ROCKRIDGE MARKET HALL
5655 College Avenue
Oakland, California 94618
888-952-4005
510-547-4005
www.markethallfoods.com
A bright, inviting shop with artisanal pastas, artichoke hearts roasted in olive oil, farro and other grains, Sicilian sea salt, regional and organic Italian olive oils, vinegars, Italian honey, prosciutto di Parma, housemade sausage, artisan breads, and a full line of cheese.

G. B. RATTO'S INTERNATIONAL MARKET
827 Washington Street
Oakland, California 94607
510-832-6503
This charming Italian market in Old Oakland has been in continuous operation since 1897. It has an outstanding cheese counter, high-quality bulk pasta, dried beans and legumes, and a rich assortment of specialty items imported from Italy and other countries.

SALUMERIA BIELLESE
376 Eighth Avenue
New York, New York 10001
212-736-7376
www.salumeriabiellese.com
Begun in 1925, this tiny meat-packing company produces 40 varieties of excellent sausages for home cooks and star chefs from coast to coast, including lamb prosciutto, *guanciale,* and exotic meats.

S.O.S. CHEFS OF NEW YORK
104 Avenue B
New York, New York 10009
212-505-5813
www.sos-chefs.com
Beyond oils and other condiments, spices, and legumes, this little shop has an exceptional variety of fresh wild mushrooms all year long and fresh truffles when in season.

SUMMERFIELD FARM
10044 James Monroe Highway
Culpeper, Virginia 22701
800-898-3276
www.summerfieldfarm.com
Jamie Nicoll raises some of the finest milk-fed veal and lamb in the world without the use of confinement or drugs.

TODARO BROTHERS
555 Second Avenue
New York, New York 10016
212-532-0633
877-472-2767
www.todarobros.com
Since 1917, this New York establishment has specialized in Italian prepared foods, pastas, cheeses, olives, and oils.

TRINACRIA MACARONI WORKS
406 North Paca Street
Baltimore, Maryland 21201
410-685-7285
Excellent, small Italian deli with lots of fans for their sausages, fresh mozzarella, prosciutto di Parma, rices, etc.

VIVANDE, INC.
2125 Fillmore Street
San Francisco, California 95115
415-346-4430
www.vivande.com
Cookbook author-chef Carlo Middione sells cheeses, oils, breads, and pastas from his San Francisco restaurant Vivande Porta Via.

ZINGERMAN'S
422 Detroit Street
Ann Arbor, Michigan 48104
888-636-8162
www.zingermans.com
Recognized as being among America's finest specialty food shops, known for service and delivering extraordinary, traditionally made foods to customers across the country. Imported pastas, oils, vinegars, saba, and almost any specialty food a cook could want.

Index

Acqua pazza, xiii, 102–103

Affogato, 198

Agnolotti Filled with Ricotta and Spinach, 78–80

Almond Cake with Roasted Apricots and Vanilla Cream, 232–233

Anchovy Vinaigrette, Chicory Salad with, 8–9

Antipasti, 2–3, 102

Apple Tart, Crustless, 218–219

Apricots
Roasted, 232, 233
Vanilla-Roasted, 208–210

Artichoke(s), xi
hearts, preparing, 69
Jerusalem, 45
in the Jewish-style, 24
John Dory with Basil and, 111–113
Soup, Creamy Sunchoke and, 44–45
Taglietelli with, 68–69

Arugula, 6
and Bibb Lettuce Salad, 5–6
Salad, Fennel, Hazelnut and, 7

Asparagus
Gemelli with, 74–75
Roasted, 160–162
Salad, Warm, 11–13

Assorted Boiled Meats, 175–176

Balsamic vinegar, 118
Chicken Marinated in, 142–143
White, 5–6

Basic Pasta, 55–56

Basic Tomato Sauce, 260

Beans, cooking, 17. *See also specific types*

Béchamel Sauce, 76–77

Beef
Minced Tenderloin of, with White Truffles, 46–48
Sliced Steak with Rosemary, 167

Beets, Roasted, with Shaved Parmigiano and Hazelnut Vinaigrette, 10

Beignets, Ricotta, with Chocolate Dipping Sauce, 220–222

Berry marmalade, 211, 223–224

Bibb Lettuce and Arugula Salad with Grape Tomatoes, Robiola Crostino, and White Balsamic Vinegar, 5–6

Blackberry Gelato, 244

Borlotti beans, 39

Braised Short Ribs, 172–174

Brick-Roasted Pheasant, 147–148

Broccoli Rabe
and Potatoes, 171
Roast Squab with Butternut Squash, Porcini Mushrooms, and, 144–146
Sautéed, Baked Polenta with Pancetta and, 94–96

Brussels Sprouts with Pancetta, 184–185

Budini, 212, 214

Butter, Truffle, 264

Butternut squash, 82
Pasta Hats, Filled with Amaretti, Parmigiano-Reggiano, and, 81–83
Roast Squab with Broccoli Rabe, Porcini Mushrooms, and, 144–146

Cake(s)
Almond, with Roasted Apricots and Vanilla Cream, 232–233
Individual Chocolate, with Fresh Raspberries, 225–227

Caponata, 103

Caramel Sauce, 234, 235

Carciofi, xi

Cheesecake, 199

Cheese pumpkins, 36

Cherry Mascarpone Tartlets, Individual, 230–231

Chestnut Honey Glazed Peaches, 156

Chicken
Marinated in Balsamic Vinegar, 142–143
Roast, 140–141
Stock, Homemade, 255
Stock, Rich, 256–257

Chickpeas, 17

Chicory Salad with Anchovy Vinaigrette, 8–9

Chitarra, 164

Chocolate
Buttercream, 215, 216
Cakes, Individual, 225–227
Cream, 238, 239

Clams
purging, 122
in Simple Broth, 32–34

Cod with Shellfish, 120–122

Condiments, 252

Cookies, Vanilla, with Chocolate Buttercream Filling, 215–217

Cooking techniques, xii–xxv

Cornmeal, 54

Couscous, Halibut with, 114–116

Creamy Artichoke and Sunchoke Soup, 44–45

Cremona-Style Mostarda, 263–264

Crêpes, Nutella-Filled, with Vanilla Gelato and Salted Hazelnuts, 234–237

Crochette, 198

Croutons, 9

Crustless Apple Tart, 218–219

Curcurbita moschata, 36

Desserts, 198–199, 233

Dried Fruit Marmelatta, 212, 214

Escarole, Savory, with Anchovies, 186

Espresso Cream, 238, 239

Farmer-Style Spinach, 188

Fava beans, 58
Gnocchi with Morels and, 90–91
Spaghetti with Grape Tomatoes and, 57–58

Fennel, 182, 183
Roasted, with Parmigiano-Reggiano, 190–191
Salad, Arugula, Hazelnut, and, 7

Fish, 102–103. *See also specific types*

Fish (*continued*)
  cooking, 102–103
  preparing, xii–xiii
  Soup, 134–135
  Stock, 254
Fisherman's Risotto, 97–99
Fried dough, 198
Fried Scamorza Cheese with Green Sauce, 20–21
Fried Zucchini Flowers with Fresh Tomato Sauce, 18–19
Fruits, xi–xii, 198. *See also specific fruits*

Game birds, 139
Garganelli, 53
Gelato, 198
  Blackberry, 244
  Mocha, 245
  Vanilla, 234–237
  Vanilla Bean, 240–241
  Wildflower Honey, 242–243
Gemelli with Asparagus, 74–75
Gigante beans, 17
Gnocchi with Morels and Fava Beans, 90–91
Goatfish, 31
Granita, Lemon, 200–202
Grape tomatoes, 60
Green Apple Sorbet, 248, 249
Green Sauce, 261
Grilled Lobster with Citrus Pesto Sauce, 125–127
Grilled Octopus Salad, 14–16
Grilled Swordfish with Artichoke Caponata, 123–124

Halibut with Couscous, 114–116
Hearty Lamb Ragout with Rigatoni, 163–164
Herbs, in desserts, 198, 233
Herbed Pork Rolls, 157
Homemade Chicken Stock, 255
Honey Glazed Peaches, 156

Ice Cream, Vanilla, with Coffee Shots, 228–229

Individual Cherry Mascarpone Tartlets, 230–231
Individual Chocolate Cakes with Fresh Raspberries, 225–227
Ingredients, xi–xii
  local, xiii–xiv
  selecting, xiv
  staples, 252
  substituting, xv

Jerusalem artichokes, 45
John Dory with Artichokes and Basil, 111–113
Johnson, Hugh, 202

Kale, Tuscan Braised, 187
Katz, Elizabeth, 199

Lamb, 139
  Ragout, Hearty, with Rigatoni, 163–164
  Roasted Rack of, with Broccoli Rabe and Potatoes and Red Wine Sauce, 168–171
  Roast Leg of, Wrapped in Pancetta, 165–166
Lasagna with Meat Sauce, 76–77
Lemon
  Granita, with Fresh Strawberry Sauce, 200–202
  Olive Oil, 253
  Pudding, Steamed, with Berry Marmalade, 211
  Tart, with Berry Marmalade, 223–224
Lentil Soup, 40–41
Lobster
  Grilled, with Citrus Pesto Sauce, 125–127
  Tagliolini with Shrimp and, 65–67

Mango Sorbet, 248, 249
Mascarpone Cream, 238, 239
Mayonnaise, Wild Mushroom, 262
Meats
  Assorted Boiled, 175–176
  browning, xiv
  cooking, 138–139
Meat Sauce, Lasagna with, 76–77

Minced Tenderloin of Beef with White Truffles, 46–48
Mocha Gelato, 245
Mollica, 9
Morel Sauce, 90–91
Moscato d'Asti Naturale, 202
Mostarda, 252
  Cremona-Style, 263–264
Mushrooms
  Black Trumpet, Roasted Pumpkin Soup with Toasted Walnuts, Brussels Sprouts, and, 35–37
  Oven-Roasted, 194–195
  Roast Squab with Butternut Squash, Broccoli Rabe, and, 144–146
  Wild, Mayonnaise, 262
My Tuscan Bean Soup with Kale and Spelt, 38–39

Nutella-Filled Crêpes with Vanilla Gelato and Salted Hazelnuts, 234–237

Octopus, Grilled, Salad, 14–16
Oils
  Lemon Olive, 253
  olive, 34
  Olive, Poached Shrimp in, 25
  reusing, 153
Olives, Taggiasca, 106
Oranges, 28
Oven-Roasted Mushrooms, 194–195
Oxtail Tortellini, 84–87

Pancetta, 182–183
  Baked Polenta with Sautéed Broccoli Rabe and, 94–96
  Brussels Sprouts with, 184–185
  Roast Leg of Lamb Wrapped in, 165–166
Pan juices, saving, 153
Pan-Roasted Salmon with Black Plums, Peaches, and Tomatoes, 128–129
Pappardelle, 53
  with Bolognese-Style Braised Rabbit and Parmigiano-Reggiano Cream, 70–71
Pasta, 52–54. *See also specific types*
  Basic, 55–56

cooking, 53

making, 52

portion sizes for, 54

sauces paired with, 53

Pasta Hats Filled with Butternut Squash,
Amaretti, and Parmigiano-Reggiano,
with Sage Butter Sauce, 81–83

Pasta Quills with San Daniele Prosciutto,
Spring Peas, and Cream, 72–73

Peaches, xii

Chestnut Honey Glazed, 156

with Pan-Roasted Salmon, 128–129

Roasted, with Streusel Topping, 206–207

Peas with Prosciutto, 189

Pescatore Sauce, 97–98

Pheasant

Brick-Roasted, 147–148

cooking, 148

Piave cheese, 64

Polenta, 54

Baked, with Sautéed Broccoli Rabe and
Pancetta, 94–96

Rabbit with Sicilian Olives and, 149–150

Soft, Robiola Cheese with Fonduta and,
92–93

Pork

pancetta, 182–183

Roasted, with Glazed Peaches, 154–156

Rolls, Herbed, 157

Potatoes

Broccoli Rabe and, 171

Rosemary Roasted, 192–193

Poultry, 138, 139. See also Chicken

Prosciutto, xi

Peas with, 189

Pumpkin, 36

Puddings, Steamed, 212–214

Roasted, Soup, 35–37

Rabbit

Braised, Bolognese-Style, Pappardelle
with Parmigiano-Reggiano Cream and,
70–71

Braised, in Oil Piedmont Style, 151–153

with Polenta and Sicilian Olives,
149–150

Radicchio rosso di Treviso, xii

Red mullet, 31

Salad, Potato, Baby Chicory and, 29–31

Red Snapper, Roasted, with Chicory and
White Beans, 130–133

Rhubarb Sorbet, 247, 249

Rich Chicken Stock, 256–257

Ricotta Beignets with Chocolate Dipping
Sauce, 220–222

Risotto, 54

Fisherman's, 97–99

Roast Chicken, 140–141

Roasted Beets with Shaved Parmigiano
and Hazelnut Vinaigrette, 10

Roasted Fennel with
Parmigiano-Reggiano, 190–191

Roasted Peaches with Streusel Topping,
206–207

Roasted Pork with Glazed Peaches,
154–156

Roasted Pumpkin Soup with Toasted
Walnuts, Brussels Sprouts, and Black
Trumpet Mushrooms, 35–37

Roasted Rack of Lamb with Broccoli Rabe
and Potatoes and Red Wine Sauce,
168–171

Roasted Red Snapper with Chicory and
White Beans, 130–133

Roast Leg of Lamb Wrapped in Pancetta,
165–166

Roast Squab with Broccoli Rabe,
Butternut Squash, and Porcini
Mushrooms, 144–146

Robiola Cheese-Filled Tortelli, 88–89

Robiola Cheese with Soft Polenta and
Fonduta, 92–93

Rosemary Roasted Potatoes, 192–193

Rosemary Salt, 253

Saba, 118

Sablée Dough, 224

Salads, 2, 195

Salmon, Pan-Roasted, with Black Plums,
Peaches, and Tomatoes, 128–129

Salmoriglio, 102

Salt, Rosemary, 253

Salumi, xi

Sauces, 252

Basic Tomato, 260

Caramel, 234, 235

Chocolate Dipping, 220–222

Citrus Pesto, 125–127

Fresh Strawberry, 200–202

Fresh Tomato, 18–19

Green, 261

Morel, 90–91

Pescatore, 97–98

Red Wine, 168–171

Salmoriglio, 102, 109–110

Sautéed Sea Scallops, Crispy Artichokes,
and Truffle Vinaigrette, 22–24

Savory Escarole with Anchovies, 186

Scamorza Cheese, Fried, with Green
Sauce, 20–21

Sea Bass

in "Crazy Water," 107–108

with Salmoriglio Sauce, 109–110

Wild Striped, Carpaccio, 104–106

Seared Veal Chop with Sweet and Sour
Cipollini Onions and Roasted
Asparagus, 160–162

Sea Scallops, Sautéed, Crispy Artichokes,
and Truffle Vinaigrette, 22–24

Semifreddo, 198

Vanilla, 203–205

Shellfish, 102–103. See also specific types

Short Ribs, Braised, 172–174

Shrimp

with Gigante Beans, 26–28

Olive Oil Poached, with Artichokes, 25

Tagliolini with Lobster and, 65–67

Sliced Steak with Rosemary, 167

Sorbet Trio, 247–249

Soups, 2

of Bitter Greens with Cheese Dumplings,
42–43

Creamy Artichoke and Sunchoke, 44–45

Fish, 134–135

Lentil, 40–41

Roasted Pumpkin, 35–37

Tuscan Bean, 38–39

South Tyrolean Venison Stew, 177–178

Spaghetti
  with Fava Beans and Grape Tomatoes,
    57–58
  with Mussels and Zucchini, 59–61
  square, 164
Spinach
  Agnolotti Filled with Ricotta and, 78–80
  Farmer-Style, 188
Squab, Roast, with Broccoli Rabe,
    Butternut Squash, and Porcini
    Mushrooms, 144–146
Staples, 252
Steak, Sliced, with Rosemary, 167
Steamed Lemon Pudding with Berry
    Marmalade, 211
Steamed Pumpkin Puddings with Dried
    Fruit Marmalade, 212–214
Stocks, 252
  Fish, 254
  Homemade Chicken, 255
  Rich Chicken, 256–257
  Veal, 258–259
Sugar, vanilla, 207
Sunchokes, 45
  Soup, Creamy Artichoke and, 44–45
Sweetbreads, 139
  Veal, with Peas and Marsala, 158–159
Sweet Mascarpone, 214
Swordfish, Grilled, with Artichoke
    Caponata, 123–124

Taggiasca olives, 106
Taglietelli with Artichokes, 68–69
Tagliolini (tagliarini), 53
  with Shrimp and Lobster, 65–67
Techniques of Italian cooking, xii–xxv
Thin Ribbon Pasta with Piave Cream,
    Speck, and Radicchio, 62–64
Tiramisù Cup, 238–239
Tomato
  grape, 60
  Sauce, Basic, 260
  Sauce, Fresh, 18–19
Tonno, xiii, 138
Topinambour, 45
Tortelli, Robiola Cheese-Filled, 88–89
Tortellini, Oxtail, 84–87

Treviso, xii
Truffle Butter, 264
Tuna with Caponata, 117–119
Tuscan Braised Kale, 187

Vanilla
  Cookies, with Chocolate Buttercream
    Filling, 215–217
  Cream, 232, 233
  extract, 241
  Frozen Yogurt, 246
  Ice Cream, with Coffee Shots, 228–229
  -Roasted Apricots, 208–210
  Semifreddo, 198, 203–205
  sugar, 207
Vanilla beans, 207, 241
  Gelato, 240–241
Veal
  Chop, Seared, with Sweet and Sour
    Cipollini Onions and Roasted
    Asparagus, 160–162
  Stock, 258–259
  Sweetbreads, with Peas and Marsala,
    158–159
Vegetables, xiii, 182–183
Venison Stew, South Tyrolean, 177–178
le verdure, 182–183
Vin Santo, 210

Warm Asparagus Salad, 11–13
Wildflower Honey Gelato, 242–243
Wild Mushroom Mayonnaise, 262
Wild Striped Sea Bass Carpaccio with
    Fennel, Tomatoes, and Ligurian Olives,
    104–106
Wines
  Moscato d'Asti Naturale, 202
  vin Santo, 210

Yogurt, Vanilla Frozen, 246

Zucchini Flowers, Fried, with Fresh
    Tomato Sauce, 18–19

cooking, 53
making, 52
portion sizes for, 54
sauces paired with, 53
Pasta Hats Filled with Butternut Squash,
Amaretti, and Parmigiano-Reggiano,
with Sage Butter Sauce, 81–83
Pasta Quills with San Daniele Prosciutto,
Spring Peas, and Cream, 72–73
Peaches, xii
Chestnut Honey Glazed, 156
with Pan-Roasted Salmon, 128–129
Roasted, with Streusel Topping, 206–207
Peas with Prosciutto, 189
Pescatore Sauce, 97–98
Pheasant
Brick-Roasted, 147–148
cooking, 148
Piave cheese, 64
Polenta, 54
Baked, with Sautéed Broccoli Rabe and
Pancetta, 94–96
Rabbit with Sicilian Olives and, 149–150
Soft, Robiola Cheese with Fonduta and,
92–93
Pork
pancetta, 182–183
Roasted, with Glazed Peaches, 154–156
Rolls, Herbed, 157
Potatoes
Broccoli Rabe and, 171
Rosemary Roasted, 192–193
Poultry, 138, 139. See also Chicken
Prosciutto, xi
Peas with, 189
Pumpkin, 36
Puddings, Steamed, 212–214
Roasted, Soup, 35–37

Rabbit
Braised, Bolognese-Style, Pappardelle
with Parmigiano-Reggiano Cream and,
70–71
Braised, in Oil Piedmont Style, 151–153
with Polenta and Sicilian Olives,
149–150

Radicchio rosso di Treviso, xii
Red mullet, 31
Salad, Potato, Baby Chicory and, 29–31
Red Snapper, Roasted, with Chicory and
White Beans, 130–133
Rhubarb Sorbet, 247, 249
Rich Chicken Stock, 256–257
Ricotta Beignets with Chocolate Dipping
Sauce, 220–222
Risotto, 54
Fisherman's, 97–99
Roast Chicken, 140–141
Roasted Beets with Shaved Parmigiano
and Hazelnut Vinaigrette, 10
Roasted Fennel with
Parmigiano-Reggiano, 190–191
Roasted Peaches with Streusel Topping,
206–207
Roasted Pork with Glazed Peaches,
154–156
Roasted Pumpkin Soup with Toasted
Walnuts, Brussels Sprouts, and Black
Trumpet Mushrooms, 35–37
Roasted Rack of Lamb with Broccoli Rabe
and Potatoes and Red Wine Sauce,
168–171
Roasted Red Snapper with Chicory and
White Beans, 130–133
Roast Leg of Lamb Wrapped in Pancetta,
165–166
Roast Squab with Broccoli Rabe,
Butternut Squash, and Porcini
Mushrooms, 144–146
Robiola Cheese-Filled Tortelli, 88–89
Robiola Cheese with Soft Polenta and
Fonduta, 92–93
Rosemary Roasted Potatoes, 192–193
Rosemary Salt, 253

Saba, 118
Sablée Dough, 224
Salads, 2, 195
Salmon, Pan-Roasted, with Black Plums,
Peaches, and Tomatoes, 128–129
Salmoriglio, 102
Salt, Rosemary, 253

Salumi, xi
Sauces, 252
Basic Tomato, 260
Caramel, 234, 235
Chocolate Dipping, 220–222
Citrus Pesto, 125–127
Fresh Strawberry, 200–202
Fresh Tomato, 18–19
Green, 261
Morel, 90–91
Pescatore, 97–98
Red Wine, 168–171
Salmoriglio, 102, 109–110
Sautéed Sea Scallops, Crispy Artichokes,
and Truffle Vinaigrette, 22–24
Savory Escarole with Anchovies, 186
Scamorza Cheese, Fried, with Green
Sauce, 20–21
Sea Bass
in "Crazy Water," 107–108
with Salmoriglio Sauce, 109–110
Wild Striped, Carpaccio, 104–106
Seared Veal Chop with Sweet and Sour
Cipollini Onions and Roasted
Asparagus, 160–162
Sea Scallops, Sautéed, Crispy Artichokes,
and Truffle Vinaigrette, 22–24
Semifreddo, 198
Vanilla, 203–205
Shellfish, 102–103. See also specific types
Short Ribs, Braised, 172–174
Shrimp
with Gigante Beans, 26–28
Olive Oil Poached, with Artichokes, 25
Tagliolini with Lobster and, 65–67
Sliced Steak with Rosemary, 167
Sorbet Trio, 247–249
Soups, 2
of Bitter Greens with Cheese Dumplings,
42–43
Creamy Artichoke and Sunchoke, 44–45
Fish, 134–135
Lentil, 40–41
Roasted Pumpkin, 35–37
Tuscan Bean, 38–39
South Tyrolean Venison Stew, 177–178

Spaghetti
  with Fava Beans and Grape Tomatoes,
    57–58
  with Mussels and Zucchini, 59–61
  square, 164
Spinach
  Agnolotti Filled with Ricotta and, 78–80
  Farmer-Style, 188
Squab, Roast, with Broccoli Rabe,
    Butternut Squash, and Porcini
    Mushrooms, 144–146
Staples, 252
Steak, Sliced, with Rosemary, 167
Steamed Lemon Pudding with Berry
    Marmalade, 211
Steamed Pumpkin Puddings with Dried
    Fruit Marmalade, 212–214
Stocks, 252
  Fish, 254
  Homemade Chicken, 255
  Rich Chicken, 256–257
  Veal, 258–259
Sugar, vanilla, 207
Sunchokes, 45
  Soup, Creamy Artichoke and, 44–45
Sweetbreads, 139
  Veal, with Peas and Marsala, 158–159
Sweet Mascarpone, 214
Swordfish, Grilled, with Artichoke
    Caponata, 123–124

Taggiasca olives, 106
Taglietelli with Artichokes, 68–69
Tagliolini (tagliarini), 53
  with Shrimp and Lobster, 65–67
Techniques of Italian cooking, xii–xxv
Thin Ribbon Pasta with Piave Cream,
    Speck, and Radicchio, 62–64
Tiramisù Cup, 238–239
Tomato
  grape, 60
  Sauce, Basic, 260
  Sauce, Fresh, 18–19
Tonno, xiii, 138
Topinambour, 45
Tortelli, Robiola Cheese-Filled, 88–89
Tortellini, Oxtail, 84–87

Treviso, xii
Truffle Butter, 264
Tuna with Caponata, 117–119
Tuscan Braised Kale, 187

Vanilla
  Cookies, with Chocolate Buttercream
    Filling, 215–217
  Cream, 232, 233
  extract, 241
  Frozen Yogurt, 246
  Ice Cream, with Coffee Shots, 228–229
  -Roasted Apricots, 208–210
  Semifreddo, 198, 203–205
  sugar, 207
Vanilla beans, 207, 241
  Gelato, 240–241
Veal
  Chop, Seared, with Sweet and Sour
    Cipollini Onions and Roasted
    Asparagus, 160–162
  Stock, 258–259
  Sweetbreads, with Peas and Marsala,
    158–159
Vegetables, xiii, 182–183
Venison Stew, South Tyrolean, 177–178
le verdure, 182–183
Vin Santo, 210

Warm Asparagus Salad, 11–13
Wildflower Honey Gelato, 242–243
Wild Mushroom Mayonnaise, 262
Wild Striped Sea Bass Carpaccio with
    Fennel, Tomatoes, and Ligurian Olives,
    104–106
Wines
  Moscato d'Asti Naturale, 202
  vin Santo, 210

Yogurt, Vanilla Frozen, 246

Zucchini Flowers, Fried, with Fresh
    Tomato Sauce, 18–19